Hugo's Simplified System

French
in Three Months

Ronald Overy and Jacqueline Lecanuet

Hugo's Language Books

A DK PUBLISHING BOOK

First American Edition, 1998
10 9 8 7 6 5 4 3 2 1

Published in the United States by
DK Publishing, Inc.
95 Madison Avenue
New York, New York 10016
Visit us on the World Wide Web at http://www.dk.com

Copyright © 1998
Dorling Kindersley Limited, London

Library of Congress Cataloging-in-Publication Data
French in three months.
        p.   cm. -- (Hugo)
        Includes index.
        ISBN 0–7894–3225–0 (alk. paper). -- ISBN 0–7894–3226–9
        (alk. paper with cassette)
        1. French Language--Textbooks for foreign speakers --
        English. I. DK Publishing, Inc. II. Series: Hugo (Series)
        PC 2129.E5F75 1998
        448.2'421 -- dc21   97–47224
                                   CIP

Set in 10/12pt Palatino by
Andrew Burrell
Reproduced, printed and bound in Italy by
L.E.G.O., Vicenza

Preface

French in Three Months has been written by two lecturers
whose combined experience in teaching French ranges from
beginners to postgraduate level. Both authors taught at the
South Bank Polytechnic, London, now the South Bank
University, where Jacqueline Lecanuet is Principal Lecturer
in French. She is a graduate of Caen and Lille Universities
and holds a post-graduate diploma in linguistics. This
revised and enlarged edition is dedicated to the memory of
her husband Ronald Overy, an inspired teacher and author
of textbooks in French, Spanish, and Russian, who died just
after completing the revision.

The book begins with an explanation of French pronunciation, as far as this is possible in print. If you are working
without a teacher, you will find that our system of "imitated
pronunciation" simplifies matters considerably. Using the
book together with our cassette recordings is an ideal
combination and provides another dimension to the course.

It has always been a principle of the Hugo method to
teach only what is essential. We assume that the student wants
to learn French from a practical angle; the lessons contain
those rules of grammar that will be of most use in this
respect. Constructions are clearly explained, and the order
in which everything is presented takes into consideration
the need for rapid progress. Each chapter includes a large
number of exercises, and the vocabulary introduced is both
practical and up-to-date. Often, in addition to testing a
grammatical point, an exercise includes specific vocabulary.
For example: Exercise 45 deals with relative pronouns and
the hotel, Exercise 57 with conjunctions and camping,
Exercise 67 with the subjunctive and space travel. The
Conversations offer examples of everyday French and,
frequently, are humorous.

3

The course finishes with a short selection of reading passages illustrating both literary and journalistic styles, all with an English translation. It is important to remember, however, that idiomatic language cannot be translated literally without the occasional appearance of some rather formal phrases.

Ideally, you should spend about an hour a day on your work (slightly less, perhaps, if you do not use the cassette recordings), although there is no hard and fast rule on this. Do as much as you feel capable of doing; if you have no special aptitude for learning languages, there is no point in forcing yourself beyond your daily capacity to assimilate new material. It is much better to learn a little at a time, and to learn that thoroughly.

Before beginning a new section or chapter, always spend ten minutes revising what you learned the day before. When studying the chapters, first read each rule or numbered section carefully and reread it to ensure that you have fully understood the grammar. Then translate the exercise(s) that follow by writing down the answers. Check these by referring to the Key at the back of the book; if you have made too many mistakes, go back over the instructions before attempting the same questions again. After you have listened to the Conversations, read them aloud and see how closely you can imitate the voices on the recording.

When the course is completed, you should have a very good understanding of the language – more than sufficient for general vacation or business purposes, and enough to lead quickly into an examination syllabus if this is your eventual aim. Remember that it is important to continue expanding your vocabulary through reading, listening to the radio, and, best of all, through visiting the country.

We hope you will enjoy *French in Three Months*, and we wish you success with your studies.

Contents

Pronunciation

French is a pleasant sounding language, but it can present one or two problems from the point of view of pronunciation. We have, however, simplified the issue by using Hugo's method of imitated pronunciation, which is sufficiently accurate to make yourself understood. Naturally, if you wish to hear perfect pronunciation, you should buy the cassette recordings that we have produced to accompany the course. These tapes allow you to hear the words and phrases as you follow them in the book.

Although French spelling appears complicated, it still remains more phonetic than that of English.

You should read through the following rules and advice on French pronunciation, but there is no need to learn the rules by heart; just refer back to them at frequent intervals and you will soon become familiar with them. In the meantime, you can start at Chapter 1 and rely on our imitated pronunciation.

Stress

Unlike English, all syllables in French words are distinctly sounded and evenly stressed, with a little more emphasis given to the last syllable. Contrast the stress in the word "important" that appears in both languages:

English: im-POR-tant
French: *ang*-por-tah*ng*

Pronunciation of vowels

a	is pronounced like "ah" in English: la (the).
à	is also pronounced like "ah": là (there).
â	is pronounced like "ah" but longer: âne (donkey).
e	in the middle of a syllable is pronounced like ai in "fair": mer (sea).
e	at the end of a syllable is pronounced like er in "her": le (the).
e	is silent at the end of a word: tasse (cup).
é	is pronounced like "ay": été (summer).
è	is pronounced like ai in "fair": père (father).
ê	is also pronounced like ai in "fair": tête (head).
i, y	are pronounced like ee in "meet": ski (skiing), y (there).
o	is pronounced like o in "not": poste (post office).
ô	is pronounced like "oh": hôtel.
u	this sound does not exist in English; say "oo" with rounded lips: vu (seen).
oi	is pronounced like "wah": roi (king).
ou	is pronounced like "oo": roue (wheel).
ai, ei	are pronounced like e in "let": laine (wool), reine (queen).
au, oeu	are pronounced like "oh": au (to the), eau (water).
eu, oeu	are pronounced like er in "her": neuf (nine), soeur (sister).

Pronunciation of consonants

French consonants are pronounced the same way as in English, but note the following:

c	before e or i sounds like "s": ceci (this).
c	elsewhere sounds like "k": car (coach).
ç	sounds like "s": ça (that).
ch	sounds like "sh": château (castle).
g	before e or i sounds like s in "measure": général.
g	elsewhere sounds like g in "go": gare (station).
h	is silent: hôtel.
j	sounds like s in "measure": je (I).
qu, q	sound like "k": qui (who).
r	is pronounced at the back of the throat; it is the sound we make when gargling: rire (to laugh).
s	at the beginning of a word sounds like "s": salle (room).
s	between two vowels sounds like "z": rose.

IMPORTANT: with the exception of c, f, l, and r, consonants are not usually pronounced when they form the last letter of a word: passeport, Paris BUT hotel, professeur

Nasal sounds

These sounds are very characteristic of the French language, but we have nasal sounds in English too. Compare: sing, sang, sung, song – remembering that the standard pronunciation gives little value to the g. French has four similar nasal sounds, which we show as ng in the "imitated pronunciation" (see p. 12):

om, on	pronounce like o*ng* in "song": nom (name), non (no).
um*, un	pronounce like u*ng* in "sung": un (one), brun (brown).
am, an em, en	pronounce like "ah*ng*": champ (field), an (year), temps (time), en (in).
im*, in, aim, ain, ein	pronounce like a*ng* in 'sang': simple (easy), vin (wine), faim (hunger), bain (bath), plein (full).
ien	pronounce like "ee-a*ng*": bien (well).

*Some French speakers make no distinction between these two sounds and pronounce them both like a*ng* in "sang."

Variations

er	at the end of a word of two syllables or more sounds like "ay": parler (to speak).
ez	at the end of a word sounds like "ay": nez (nose).
ail	at the end of a word sounds like "ah'ee': travail (work).
eil, eille	sound like "a'ee": soleil (sun), bouteille (bottle).
ill	usually sounds like "ee'y": billet (ticket).
gn	sounds like ni in "onion": signal.

Liaison

The French like their language to flow smoothly. For this reason, if a word beginning with a vowel or a silent h follows a word ending in a consonant, this consonant is linked to the beginning of the second word:

nous‿avons (noo zah-vo*ng*), we have
un petit‿enfant (u*ng* p'tee tah*ng*-fah*ng*), a small child

When carried over in this way,

s, x   sound like "z": deux‿ans (de*r* zah*ng*), two years.

d   sounds like "t": un grand‿arbre (u*ng* grah*ng* tahbr), a tall tree.

f   sounds like "v": neuf‿heures (ne*r* ve*rr*), nine hours.

Accents

There are three accents in French: the acute (´), found on the letter e; the grave (`), found on a, e, and u; the circumflex (^), found on any vowel. There is also the cedilla (͵), found only underneath the letter c.

The function of the accents is:

a) to modify the sound of a letter. The unaccented e sounds like er in "her," the é acute sounds like ay in "say," and the è grave sounds like ai in "fair."

The c which would be hard before an a or o (as in "car") is softened to sound like s in "sit" when it has a cedilla added (garçon, "boy").

b) to distinguish between words having the same spelling but a different meaning. For example, la (the), là (there); ou (or), où (where); sur (on), sûr (sure).

The Imitated Pronunciation

Pronounce all syllables as if they formed part of an
English word, giving equal stress to each syllable, but
note the following:

ng (italics) must never be pronounced; these letters merely
indicate that the preceding vowel has a nasal
sound.

e*r* (r italics) do not pronounce the r; this syllable sounds like
er in "her."

zh sounds like s in "measure."

ü no equivalent in English; round your lips and
say "ee."

o sounds like o in "not."

oh sounds like o in "note."

The French alphabet

This is the same as in English, but K and W are not used
much. You should know how to pronounce the letters in
case you have to spell out your name to a French receptionist:
H-A-L-E-Y sounded as "ahsh ah el er ee-grek" will make
sense to her, the English version would not.

A (ah)	H (ahsh)	O (oh)	V (vay)
B (bay)	I (ee)	P (pay)	W (doobl-vay)
C (say)	J (zhee)	Q (kü)	X (eeks)
D (day)	K (kah)	R (airr)	Y (ee-grek)
E (er)	L (el)	S (ess)	Z (zed)
F (ef)	M (em)	T (tay)	
G (zhay)	N (en)	U (ü)	

Chapter 1

In this first lesson you'll learn some basic but extremely important elements of grammar, such as:

- *how to say "the," "a," and "some"*
- *how to recognize whether a noun is masculine or feminine, and which article to use with each gender*
- *formation of the plural*
- *how to say "I, "you," "he," "she," "it," "we," "they"*
- *simple greetings and forms of address*
- *the present tense of "**avoir**," "to have"*
- *formation of the negative*

1 Articles

In French all nouns are either masculine or feminine and articles ("the," "a," "some") must agree in gender and number with the noun to which they refer.

"The" is expressed by:

le *(m. sing.)*	**le passeport** the passport
la *(f. sing.)*	**la cassette** the cassette
l' (before a vowel or h*)	**l'alcool** the alcohol
	l'hôtel the hotel
les *(m. & f. pl.)*	**les passeports** the passports

*A few words beginning with h take **le, la.**

"A" is expressed by:

un *(m. sing.)*	**un chéquier** a checkbook
une *(f. sing.)*	**une cigarette** a cigarette

"Some" or "any" is expressed by:

du *(m. sing.)*	**du vin** some wine
de la *(f. sing.)*	**de la bière** some beer
de l' (before a vowel or h)	**de l'alcool** some alcohol
des *(m. & f. pl.)*	**des cassettes** some cassettes

Note: **du** is actually a contraction of **de** and **le**, and **des** is a contraction of **de** and **les**.

Sometimes "some" and "any" are omitted in English, but they must always be expressed in French:

we have wine **nous avons du vin**

IMITATED PRONUNCIATION (1): le*r* pahs-porr; lah kah-set; lahl-kol; loh-tel; lay pahs-porr; u*ng* shek-yay; ün see-gah-ret; dü va*ng*; de*r* lah bee-airr; de*r* lahl-kol; day kah-set; noo zah-vo*ng* dü va*ng*.

2 Nouns

Unfortunately, there are few rules that can help determine the gender of French nouns. The best rule of all is to learn each noun and its gender together. Generally speaking, -e and -ion are feminine endings, although there are exceptions. Nouns denoting male persons are masculine and those which refer to female persons are feminine:

le monsieur gentleman
le journal newspaper
le parfum perfume

le magnétophone tape recorder
le château castle
le neveu nephew
le prix price
l'autobus *(m.)* bus

la dame lady
la valise suitcase
la station station

le journaliste male journalist
la journaliste female journalist

Occasionally only one gender exists and this has to be used irrespective of the sex of the person:

le professeur (teacher) is always masculine
la personne (person) is always feminine

IMITATED PRONUNCIATION (2): mers-yer; zhoor-nahl; pahr-fung; man-yay-to-fon; shah-toh; ner-ver; pree; oh-toh-büs; dahm; vah-leez; stahs-yong; zhoor-nah-leest; pro-fess-err; pairr-sonn.

2a Plural of nouns

The plural is formed:

a) by adding **s**

magnétophone (tape recorder) becomes **magnétophones**

b) by adding **x** to words ending in **au** or **eu**

château (castle) becomes **châteaux**
neveu (nephew) becomes **neveux**

c) by changing the ending **al** to **aux**

journal (newspaper) becomes **journaux**

Words ending in **s** and **x** do not change: **autobus** (bus or buses); **prix** (price or prices).

IMITATED PRONUNCIATION (2a): man-yay-to-fon; shah-toh; ner-ver; zhoor-nahl; zhoor-noh; oh-toh-büs; pree.

Exercise 1

Translate:

1 the passport
2 the hotel
3 the suitcase
4 a station
5 a tape recorder
6 a checkbook
7 a person
8 the journalists
9 the prices
10 some beer
11 some wine
12 some cassettes
13 some newspapers
14 some buses

3 Subject pronouns

singular		*plural*	
je	I	**nous**	we
tu	you *(familiar)*	**vous**	you *(familiar)*
vous	you *(formal)*	**vous**	you *(formal)*
il	he, it *(m.)*	**ils**	they *(m.)*
elle	she, it *(f.)*	**elles**	they *(f.)*

Note: je becomes j' before a vowel or h.

3a Forms of Address

Sometimes English can be a very straightforward
language. Whether we are addressing a dog, our husband
or wife, or the President, we use the same word "you."
In French, it's not quite as simple because we have two
words for "you" – **tu** and **vous** – and to use them incorrectly
would be a very serious mistake.

The French use **tu** when talking to animals, children, very
close friends, and relatives. Note, however, that although
you use **tu** to one child, you would address more than one
child as **vous**. Teenagers use **tu** with each other, even on
first meeting.

In all other cases we use the more formal **vous**. Unless we
indicate otherwise (by putting in brackets the word
"familiar"), we would like you to use **vous** in all the exercises
in this book.

Note also that what has been said about **tu** and **vous** also
applies to **te** (you), **ton** (your), **votre** (your), etc.

You are no doubt already vaguely familiar with the words **Monsieur**, **Madame**, and **Mademoiselle**; they mean Mr., Mrs., and Miss and are placed, as in English, before a last name:

Monsieur Dupont, Madame Duval, Mademoiselle Martin.

The French also use these words a great deal in formal conversation, without a name following:

Bonjour, Monsieur. Good morning, good afternoon (to a man).
Bonsoir, Madame. Good evening (to a woman).
Au revoir, Mademoiselle. Goodbye (to a young woman).

Monsieur, **Madame**, and **Mademoiselle** also have a plural form: **Messieurs, Mesdames, Mesdemoiselles.**

IMITATED PRONUNCIATION (3, 3a): zher; tü; voo; eel; el; noo; voo; voo; eel; el; mers-yer dü-pong; mah-dahm dü-vahl; mahd-mwah-zel mahr-tang; bong-zhoor, mers-yer; bong-swahr, mah-dahm; orr-vwahrr, mahd-mwah-zel; mays-yer; may-dahm; mayd-mwah-zel.

4 The verb "avoir" (to have)

This is one of the most important French verbs, and it should be learned thoroughly.

Present tense

j'ai	I have
tu as	you have *(familiar sing.)*
il a, elle a	he has, she has
nous avons	we have
vous avez	you have *(formal, sing. and pl.)*
ils ont, elles ont	they *(m.)* have, they *(f.)* have

Vocabulary

Study these words:

le livre	book
l'appareil-photo *(m.)*	camera
le disque	record
la carte	map, card
la clé	key
la voiture	car
la radio	radio
oui	yes
non	no
et	and

IMITATED PRONUNCIATION (4): ah-vwahr; zhay; tü ah; eel ah; el ah; noo zah-vong; voo zah-vay; eel zong; el zong; leevr; ah-pah-ray'ee fo-toh; deesk; kahrt; klay; vwah-tür; rad-yoh; wee; nong; ay.

Exercise 2

Answer the questions as follows:

Pierre a du vin?	Does Pierre have any wine?
Oui, il a du vin.	Yes, he has some wine.

1 Nicole a un journal?
2 Sophie et Pierre ont une voiture?
3 Vous avez une radio?
4 Vous avez une carte?
5 Nous avons une clé?
6 J'ai un disque?

Notice that we can ask questions simply by using a rising intonation.

5 The negative

"Not" is expressed by the two words **ne … pas; ne** is placed before the verb and **pas** after; **ne** becomes **n'** before a vowel or h:

je n'ai pas	I have not
il n'a pas	he has not
elle n'a pas	she has not
nous n'avons pas	we have not
vous n'avez pas	you have not *(formal, sing. and pl.)*
ils n'ont pas	they *(m.)* have not
elles n'ont pas	they *(f.)* have not

The singular familiar form **tu as** becomes **tu n'as pas.**

After a negative **un, une, du, de la, de l'**, and **des** change to **de (d'** before a vowel or h).

J'ai de la bière.	I have some beer.
Je n'ai pas de bière.	I don't have any beer.

IMITATED PRONUNCIATION (5): zher nay pah; eel nah pah; el nah pah; noo nah-vong pah; voo nah-vay pah; eel nong pah; el nong pah; tü nah pah; zhay der lah bee-airr; zher nay pah der bee-airr.

Exercise 3

Answer the questions as follows:

Vous avez une voiture?	Do you have a car?
Non, je n'ai pas de voiture.	No, I don't have a car.

1 Vous avez une valise?
2 Vous avez un passeport?
3 Nous avons du vin?
4 Nous avons un livre?
5 Paul a des disques?
6 Anne-Marie a une radio?
7 J'ai des journaux?
8 Elles ont un appareil-photo?

Exercise 4

Translate:

1 I have a tape recorder.
2 I do not have any keys.
3 We have a suitcase.
4 She has some alcohol.
5 He does not have a newspaper.
6 They (*m.*) have some cassettes.
7 They (*f.*) do not have any maps.
8 You do not have a check–book.
9 Do you have a camera?
10 Do you have any records?
11 Do you have any books?
12 Do you have a radio?

Vocabulary

à	at, to
au (à + le = au)	at the
le contrôle	control, check
le policier	policeman
le douanier	customs officer
l'instant (*m.*)	moment
le miracle	miracle
la douane	customs
le/la touriste	tourist
déclarer	to declare
c'est	this is, that is
s'il vous plaît	please
voici	here is, here are
où	where
très	very
grave	serious
quelque chose	something
mais	but
mon Dieu	good heavens
aussi	also

IMITATED PRONUNCIATION: ah; oh; kong-trohl; po-lees-yay; dwahn-yay; ang-stahng; mee-rahkl; dwahn; too-reest; day-klah-ray; say; seel voo play; vwah-see; oo; tray; grahv; kel-ker shohz; may; mong dyer; oh-see.

CONVERSATION

Au contrôle des passeports

Policier   Passeport, s'il vous plaît, Madame.

Touriste   Un instant, s'il vous plaît.
(She searches in her pocketbook.)
Le passeport? Où est le passeport? Mon
Dieu!   J'ai un chéquier, un livre, une carte
de France, une cassette, des clés, des
cigarettes mais ... je n'ai pas de passeport!

À la douane

Douanier   Vous avez quelque chose à déclarer?

Touriste   Oui, je n'ai pas de passeport.

Douanier   Vous n'avez pas de passeport? C'est très grave.
Vous avez de l'alcool?

Touriste   Oui, j'ai du vin.

Douanier   Vous avez du parfum?

Touriste   Non, je n'ai pas de parfum.

Douanier   Vous avez des cigarettes?

Touriste   Oui, j'ai des cigarettes. J'ai aussi un
appareil-photo, un magnétophone et des
cassettes.
*(The customs officer asks her to open the
suitcase.)*

Douanier   Voici le vin, voici le magnétophone,
l'appareil-photo, les cassettes, les cigarettes,
un journal, un livre et ... miracle – voici le
passeport!

TRANSLATION

At Passport Control

Immigration Officer   Passport please, Madam.

Tourist   One moment, please.
(She searches in her pocketbook.)
The passport? Where's the passport?
Good heavens! I have a checkbook,
a book, a map of France, a cassette,
some keys, some cigarettes but ...
I have no passport!

At Customs

Customs Officer   Do you have anything to declare?

Tourist   Yes, I don't have a passport.

Customs Officer   You've no passport? That's very
serious. Do you have any alcohol?

Tourist   Yes, I have some wine.

Customs Officer   Do you have any perfume?

Tourist   No, I haven't got any perfume.

Customs Officer   Do you have any cigarettes?

Tourist   Yes, I have some cigarettes. I also
have a camera, a tape recorder, and
some cassettes.
*(The customs officer asks her to
open the suitcase.)*

Customs Officer   Here's the wine, here's the tape recorder, the camera, the cassettes, the
cigarettes, a newspaper, a book, and
surprise, surprise ... here's the
the passport!

Chapter 2

Continuing with the basic essentials, you'll now learn:

- *how to say "I am," "you are,"etc. – the present tense of "être"*
- *some common adjectives, and how they must agree in number and gender with the noun to which they are attached*
- *some regular verbs (those ending in "–er" and their present tense formations)*
- *a variety of ways to frame a question*
- *numbers 0–15*

6 The verb "être"(to be)

This is another very important verb and should be learned thoroughly.

Present tense

je suis	I am
tu es	you are (*familiar sing.*)
il est	he is
elle est	she is
nous sommes	we are
vous êtes	you are
ils sont	they are (*m.*)
elles sont	they are (*f.*)

IMITATED PRONUNCIATION (6): zher swee; tü ay; eel ay; el ay; noo som; voo zet; eel song; el song.

Vocabulary

Study these professions:

le médecin	doctor
le banquier	banker
le pilote	pilot
le professeur	teacher
l'avocat *(m.)*	lawyer
l'avocate *(f.)*	lawyer
l'hôtesse de l'air	flight attendant
le/la journaliste	journalist
le/la secrétaire	secretary
l'astronaute *(m. or f.)*	astronaut

Note: when talking about their professions, the French omit the "a" and say "I am doctor," "I am pilot," etc.
je suis médecin, je suis pilote.

IMITATED PRONUNCIATION: med-sa*ng*; bah*ng*k-yay; pee-lot; pro-fess-e*rr*; ah-vo-kah; ah-vo-kaht; oh-tess-de*r*-lairr; zhoor-nah-leest; se*r*-kray-tairr; ah-stro-noht.

Exercise 5

Translate:

1 I am a doctor.
2 He is a pilot.
3 She is a journalist.
4 We are bankers.
5 You *(m.)* are a lawyer.
6 They are flight attendants
7 They *(m.)* are astronauts.

7 Adjectives

French adjectives have both a masculine and a feminine form, singular and plural. The feminine is normally formed by adding e (words already ending in e do not change). In the plural we usually add s:

Il est intelligent. He is intelligent.
Elle est intelligente. She is intelligent.
Je suis grand. I *(m.)* am tall.
Je suis grande. I *(f.)* am tall.
Ils sont petits. They *(m.)* are small.
Elles sont petites. They *(f.)* are small.

Note: the addition of the **e** results in the preceding consonant being pronounced.

Adjectives ending in x change the x to se in the feminine: **dangereux** (dangerous) becomes **dangereuse**.

IMITATED PRONUNCIATION (7): ang-tel-ee-zhahng; ang-tel-ee-zhahngt; grahng; grahngd; p'tee; p'teet; dahng-zher-rer; dahng-zher-rerz.

Vocabulary

riche	rich	**stupide**	stupid
pauvre	poor	**poli**	polite
facile	easy	**impoli**	impolite
difficile	difficult	**heureux**	happy
intéressant	interesting	**malheureux**	unhappy
ennuyeux	boring	**bon, bonne** *(f.)*	good
intelligent	intelligent	**mauvais**	bad

Additional rules for forming the feminine of adjectives:
a) final f changes to **ve: attentif, attentive** *(f.)* – attentive
b) final er changes to **ère: premier, première** *(f.)* – first
c) final et changes to **ète: secret, secrète** *(f.)* – secret

IMITATED PRONUNCIATION: reesh; pohvr; fah-seel;
dee-fee-seel; a*ng*-tay-ress-ah*ng*; ah*ng*-nwee-yer; a*ng*-tel-ee-zhah*ng*;
stü-peed; po-lee; a*ng*-po-lee; er-rer; mahl-er-rer; bo*ng*; bonn;
moh-vay; ah-tah*ng*-teef; ah-tah*ng*-teev; pre*r*m-yay; pre*r*m-yairr;
se*r*kray; se*r*kret.

Exercise 6

Give the opposite of:

1 Le banquier est riche.
2 La secrétaire est intelligente.
3 Les médecins sont heureux.
4 Les journaux sont intéressants.
5 Le vin est bon.
6 Le livre est facile.
7 L'hôtesse de l'air es polie.
8 La bière est mauvaise.

---

8 Regular verbs ending in -er

The infinitive of most French verbs ends in **-er**:

préparer	to prepare
habiter	to live
travailler	to work
parler	to speak
pratiquer	to practice
regarder	to watch
écouter	to listen (to)

We form the present tense by removing the **-er** from the infinitive and adding:

je	-e	nous	-ons
tu	-es	vous	-ez
il/elle	-e	ils/elles	-ent

je parle	I speak
tu parles	you speak *(fam.)*
il parle	he speaks
elle parle	she speaks
nous parlons	we speak
vous parlez	you speak
ils parlent	they speak *(m.)*
elles parlent	they speak *(f.)*

The French **je parle, il parle**, etc., translates all three forms of the English present tense, i.e., I speak, I do speak, I am speaking.

IMITATED PRONUNCIATION (8): pray-pah-ray; ah-bee-tay; trah-vah′ee-yay; pahr-lay; prah-tee-kay; rer-gahr-day; ay-koo-tay; zher pahrl; tü pahrl; eel pahrl; el pahrl; noo pahr-long; voo pahr-lay; eel pahrl; el pahrl.

Vocabulary

à	in, at
voyager	to travel
	(**nous voyageons;** see section 81 for details of spelling changes.)
le sport	sport
la langue	language
la télévision	television
la radio	radio
l'enquête *(f.)*	survey
deux	two

IMITATED PRONUNCIATION: ah; vwah-yah-zhay; sporr; lahngg; tay-lay-vee-zee-ong; rahd-yoh; ahng-ket; der.

Exercise 7

Complete these sentences:

1 Nous (live) à Versailles.
2 Elle (works) à Nice.
3 Il (travels).
4 Je (speak) deux langues.
5 Elles (practice) un sport.
6 Ils (watch) la télévision.
7 Vous (listen to) la radio.
8 Nous (prepare) une enquête.

9 The interrogative

In French you can ask a question:

(a) by using a rising intonation. Contrast:

Vous parlez français.
　You speak French. (statement)
Vous parlez français?
　Do you speak French? (question)

(b) by using **est-ce que (est-ce qu'** before a vowel or h):

Est-ce que nous travaillons?
　Are we working?
Est-ce qu'elle écoute la radio?
　Is she listening to the radio?

c) by putting the pronoun after the verb:

Voyagez-vous beaucoup?
　Do you travel a great deal?

In this case, if the third person singular of the verb ends in a vowel, a **t** is inserted between it and the pronoun: **Fume-t-il?** (Does he smoke?).

Note: (a) and (b) are less formal than (c) and are used more in the spoken language.

Vocabulary

téléphoner	to call (on the phone)
réserver	to reserve
exporter	to export
importer	to import
voter	to vote
inviter à dîner	to invite to dinner
il y a	there is, there are
l'hôtel *(m.)*	hotel
le directeur	director
l'ordinateur *(m.)*	computer
le président	President
l'agent *(m.)*	agent
le mousquetaire	musketeer
le pays	country
le marché	market
juillet *(m.)*	July
la chambre	bedroom
la voiture	car
la date	date
la prise	taking, storming
la Bastille	Bastille
secret	secret
commun	common
finalement	finally
dans	in
de	of
en France	in France, to France

IMITATED PRONUNCIATION (9): frah*ng*-say; ess-k*er*; boh-koo; füm-teel; tay-lay-fo-nay; ray-zairr-vay; eks-porr-tay; a*ng*-porr-tay; vo-tay; a*ng*-vee-tay ah dee-nay; eel yah; oh-tel; dee-rek-t*err*; orr-dee-nah-t*err*; pr*er*m-yay mee-neestr; ah-zhah*ng*; moo-sk*er*-tairr; pay-ee; mahr-shay; zhwee-yay; shah*ng*br; vwah-tür; daht; preez; bah-stee-y; s*er*-kray; ko-mu*ng*; fee-nahl-mah*ng*; dah*ng*; der; ah*ng* frah*ng*s.

Exercise 8

Using est-ce que, ask your friend whether he/she ...

1 is calling the hotel. (say to the hotel)
2 is reserving a room.
3 is inviting the director to dinner.

Using a rising intonation, ask about Nicole ...

4 Is she intelligent?
5 Is she interesting?
6 Is she tall?

Using the inverted form, ask about Peter ...

7 Does he export computers to France?
8 Does he import cars?
9 Does he vote for the President?

10 Numerals

Here are the numbers 0 – 15:

0	**zéro**	8	**huit**
1	**un**	9	**neuf**
2	**deux**	10	**dix**
3	**trois**	11	**onze**
4	**quatre**	12	**douze**
5	**cinq**	13	**treize**
6	**six**	14	**quatorze**
7	**sept**	15	**quinze**

IMITATED PRONUNCIATION: zay-roh; ung; der; trwah; kahtr; sangk; sees; set; weet, nerf; dees; ongz; dooz; trez; kah-torrz; kangz.

Exercise 9

Complete the following, writing the answers in words:

a	7 + 2 =		e	10 + 5 =
b	8 − 6 =		f	14 − 2 =
c	3 x 4 =		g	2 x 7 =
d	2 + 3 =		h	2 + 1 =

Complete the following as above:

1 Il y a _____ jours dans la semaine.
2 James Bond, agent secret _____ .
3 La date de la prise de la Bastille: le _____ juillet.
4 Les Trois Mousquetaires sont finalement _____ .
5 Il y a _____ mois dans l'année.

Vocabulary

sur	on
pour	for
beaucoup	a lot
seulement	only
souvent	often
jamais	never
plusieurs	several
anglais	English
le jogging	jogging
l'agence *(f.)*	agency
la publicité	advertising
la question	question
les affaires *(f.)*	business
faire	to do, to make

IMITATED PRONUNCIATION: sürr; poorr; boh-koo; serl-mah*ng*; soo-vahng; zhah-may; plüz-y*err*; ah*ng*-glay; zhog-i*ng*; ah-zhah*ng*s; pü-blee-see-tay; kest-yo*ng*; ah-fairr; fairr.

CONVERSATION

A French radio reporter is preparing a survey on the French. He's interviewing passersby in the street.

Journaliste	Pardon Madame, vous êtes Française?
Passante	Oui, je suis Française.
Journaliste	Je prépare une enquête sur les Français. J'ai sept questions.
Passante	Oui.
Journaliste	Vous habitez à Paris?
Passante	Non, j'habite à Versailles.
Journaliste	Vous travaillez à Paris?
Passante	Oui, je travaille pour une agence de publicité.
Journaliste	Est-ce que vous voyagez beaucoup?
Passante	Oui, je voyage pour affaires.
Journaliste	Est-ce que vous parlez plusieurs langues?
Passante	Deux seulement, français et anglais.
Journaliste	Pratiquez-vous un sport?
Passante	Oui, je fais du jogging.
Journaliste	Regardez-vous la télévision?
Passante	Oui, souvent.
Journaliste	Vous écoutez la radio?
Passante	Jamais!

Note: except when we refer to the people of the country, adjectives denoting nationality do not take a capital letter; **un hôtel français**, **je parle anglais**, *but* **les Français**, the French.

TRANSLATION

Journalist	Excuse me Madam, are you French?
Passerby	Yes, I'm French.
Journalist	I'm preparing a survey on the French ... I've seven questions.
Passerby	Yes.
Journalist	Do you live in Paris?
Passerby	No, I live in Versailles.
Journalist	Do you work in Paris?
Passerby	Yes, I work for an advertising agency.
Journalist	Do you travel a great deal?
Passerby	Yes, I travel on business.
Journalist	Do you speak several languages?
Passerby	Only two, French and English.
Journalist	Do you practice a sport?
Passerby	Yes, I jog.
Journalist	Do you watch television?
Passerby	Yes, often.
Journalist	Do you listen to the radio?
Passerby	Never!

Chapter 3

This chapter includes the following grammar:

- *regular verbs ending in "–ir" and their present tense*
- *demonstrative adjectives ("this," "that," "these," "those")*
- *more about the formation of negatives*
- *using interrogative words ("who?/what?/where?/when?/ why?/ which?" etc.)*
- *the imperative in its simplest form*

11 Regular verbs ending in -ir

The infinitive of a large number of French verbs ends in -**ir**:

finir	to finish
garantir	to guarantee
choisir	to choose
grossir	to put on weight
maigrir	to lose weight
remplir	to fill
réussir	to succeed

We form the present tense by removing the -**ir** from the infinitive and adding:

je	-is	**nous**	-issons
tu	-is	**vous**	-issez
il/elle	-it	**ils/elles**	-issent

je finis	I finish
tu finis	you finish
il finit	he finishes
elle finit	she finishes
nous finissons	we finish
vous finissez	you finish
ils finissent (*m.*)	they finish
elles finissent (*f.*)	they finish

Note: the singular familiar form **tu finis** ("you finish")
should be used only with close friends, children, and animals.

Vocabulary

le rapport	report
le magnétoscope	VCR
le gâteau	cake
le verre	glass
l'occasion (*f.*)	opportunity
saisir	to seize

IMITATED PRONUNCIATION (11): fee-neerr; gah-rah*ng*-teerr;
shwah-zeerr; groh-seerr; may-greerr; rah*ng*-pleerr; ray-ü-seerr;
fee-nee; fee-nee; fee-nee; fee-nee-song; fee-nee-say; fee-neess;
rah-porr; man-yay-to-skop; gah-toh; vairr; o-kahz-yo*ng*;
say-zeerr.

Exercise 10

Translate:

1 I am finishing the report.
2 We guarantee the VCR.
3 She chooses a cake.
4 He is putting on weight.
5 They (*f.*) are losing weight.
6 They (*m.*) are filling the glasses.
7 We seize the opportunity.

12 Demonstrative adjectives

Both "this" and "that" are expressed by:

ce *(m. sing.)*	**ce train**	this/that train
cet *(m. sing.)*	**cet hélicoptère**	this/that helicopter
before a vowel or h		
cette *(f. sing.)*	**cette voiture**	this/that car

Both "these"' and "those" are expressed by:

ces *(m. & f. pl.)*	**ces avions**	these/those planes

If a distinction needs to be made between "this" and "that" or "these" and "those," we can add **-ci** (short for **ici** "here") and **-là** ("there") to the noun:

ce train-ci	this train
ce train-là	that train

Vocabulary

le guichet	ticket office
l'ascenseur *(m.)*	elevator
le compartiment	compartment
le billet	ticket
la gare	train station
la place	seat
rapide	fast
important	important
fermé	closed
cher, chère *(f.)*	expensive
plein	full
réservé	reserved
occupé	occupied
valable	valid

IMITATED PRONUNCIATION (12): ser tra*ng*;
set ay-lee-kop-tairr; set vwah-türr; say zahv-yo*ng*; gee-shay;
ah-sah*ng*-serr; ko*ng*-pahr-tee-mah*ng*; bee-yay; gahr; plahs;
rah-peed; *ang*-por-tah*ng*; fairr-may; shairr; pla*ng*; ray-zairr-vay;
o-kü-pay; vah-lahbl.

Exercise 11

Translate:

1 This train is fast.
2 This station is important.
3 This ticket office is closed.
4 That car is expensive.
5 That elevator is full.
6 These seats are reserved.
7 These compartments are occupied.
8 Those tickets are valid.

---

13 Expressions with "avoir" (to have)

In French there are a number of expressions with avoir
"to have" that would be expressed in English with "to be":

avoir faim	to be hungry
avoir soif	to be thirsty
avoir chaud	to be warm
avoir froid	to be cold
avoir raison	to be right
avoir tort	to be wrong

avoir is also used in connection with age:

Il a douze ans. He is twelve. (lit. "He has twelve years.")

IMITATED PRONUNCIATION: ah-vwahr fa*ng*; swahf; shoh;
frwah; ray-zo*ng*; torr; ah*ng*.

Exercise 12

Give the opposite of:

1 J'ai faim.   4 Nous avons soif.
2 Il a raison.   5 Ils ont tort.
3 Elle a chaud.   6 Elles ont froid.

14 Negatives

We have already seen that "not" is expressed by putting **ne (n')** before the verb and **pas** after:

Je ne travaille pas. I do not work.
Il n'écoute pas. He is not listening.

Here are some more negatives and model sentences:

ne ... jamais   never
ne ... rien   nothing
ne ... personne no one
ne ... plus   no longer, no more

Il ne travaille jamais. He never works.
Elle n'exporte rien. She exports nothing.
Ils n'invitent personne. They invite no one.
Je ne fume plus. I no longer smoke.

Note:
a) **rien** and **personne** can also begin a sentence:

Rien n'est cher. Nothing is expensive.
Personne ne fume ici. No one smokes here.

b) after a negative **un, une, du, de la, de l', des**, change to **de (d')**:

Je mange de la salade. I eat salad.
Je ne mange jamais de salade. I never eat salad.

Vocabulary

l'électrophone *(m.)*	record player
le fromage	cheese
l'homme d'affaires	businessman
la glace	ice cream
la diététicienne	dietitian
manger	to eat
rencontrer	to meet
en	in, by

IMITATED PRONUNCIATION (14): ner; zhah-may; ree-a*ng*; pairr-sonn; plü; ay-lek-tro-fon; fro-mahzh; om dah-fairr; glahs; dyay-tay-tees-yen; mah*ng*-zhay; rah*ng*-ko*ng*-tray.

Exercise 13

Answer the questions using "not," as follows:

Vous voyagez en voiture? Do you travel by car?
Non, je ne voyage pas en voiture. No, I don't travel by car.

1 Vous travaillez?
2 Vous écoutez?
3 Vous avez faim?

Now answer using "never":

4 Est-ce que vous choisissez du fromage?
5 Est-ce que vous téléphonez?
6 Est-ce que vous avez froid?

Now answer using "nothing":

7 Mange-t-il une glace?
8 Prépare-t-elle un rapport?
9 Exporte-t-il des électrophones?

Now answer using "no one":

10 Nous invitons des hommes d'affaires?
11 Nous choisissons Paul?
12 Nous rencontrons la diététicienne?

Now answer using "no longer":

13 Est-ce qu'ils ont une voiture?
14 Est-ce qu'elles habitent à Paris?
15 Est-ce qu'elles travaillent?

15 Interrogatives

You will need to know how to ask questions in French:

où? where?
Où est-ce que vous habitez?
  Where do you live?

quand? when?
Quand écoutez-vous la radio?
  When do you listen to the radio?

comment? how?
Comment allez-vous?
  How are you? (literally: How do you go?)

qui? who? whom?
Qui parle français? Who speaks French?
Qui est-ce qu'elle invite? Whom is she inviting?

pourquoi? why?
Pourquoi téléphone-t-elle?
  Why is she calling?

Note: the reply to **pourquoi** is **parce que** "because."

quel *(m.)*? **quelle** *(f.)*?
quels *(m. pl.)*? **quelles** *(f. pl.)*?   which (what)?
Quelle chambre réservons-nous?
  Which room are we reserving?

combien? how much? how many?
Combien coûte ce disque?
  How much does this record cost?
Combien de fromage désirez-vous?
  How much cheese do you want?
Combien de trains y a-t-il?
  How many trains are there?

Note: **combien** takes **de (d')** when followed by a noun.

que (qu' before a vowel) or **qu'est-ce que**   what?
Que mangez-vous? *or* **Qu'est-ce que vous mangez?**
  What are you eating?

Note the word order in the above two questions.

Vocabulary

le film	movie
le soir	evening
le franc	franc
allemand	German
espagnol	Spanish
bien	well
merci	thank you
chercher	to look for

IMITATED PRONUNCIATION (15): oo; kah*ng*; ko-mah*ng*;
ko-mah*ng* tah-lay voo; kee; poorr-kwah; pahr-sk*er*; kel;
ko*ng*-bee-a*ng*; koot; deesk; day-zee-ray voo; yah-teel; k*er*;
kess-k*er*; mah*ng*-zhay; feelm; swahr; frah*ng*; ahl-mah*ng*;
ess-pan-yol; bee-a*ng*; mairr-see; shairr-shay.

Exercise 14

Below are ten replies. What were the questions? The important words are printed in italics.

1 Je travaille *à Paris*.
2 Je regarde le film *ce soir*.
3 *Bien*, merci.
4 *Pierre* téléphone.
5 Ils cherchent *Nicole*.
6 Parce que *j'ai faim*.
7 Je parle *espagnol et allemand*.
8 J'ai *quatre* cassettes.
9 Ce journal coûte *six francs*.
10 J'exporte *des magnétoscopes*.

16 The imperative

Occasionally you will need to ask or tell people to do things. Simply omit the **vous**, **tu**, or **nous** from the present tense:

Téléphonez.	Call (on the phone).
Choisissez.	Choose.
Invitons Paul.	Let's invite Paul.
Ne téléphonez pas.	Don't call (on the phone).
N'invitons pas Paul.	Let's not invite Paul.

Note: the final s of **-er** verbs is dropped in the familiar singular imperative:

Choisis.	Choose.
Finis.	Finish.
Téléphone.	Call (on the phone).

You may wish to add **s'il vous plaît** or **s'il te plaît** *(fam. sing.)* "please" to the imperative.

44

Vocabulary

les bagages *(m.)*	luggage
la méthode	method
trop	too much, too many
monter	to bring up, to take up
acheter	to buy

Note: in the present tense of the verb **acheter** a grave accent is introduced in the singular and in the third person plural. This affects the pronunciation. A more detailed explanation of this can be found in section 81 "Spelling changes":

j'achète	**nous achetons**
tu achètes	**vous achetez**
il achète	
elle achète	
ils achètent	
elles achètent	

IMITATED PRONUNCIATION (16): bah-gahzh; may-tod; troh; mong-tay; ahsh-tay; zhah-shet; tü ah-shet; eel ah-shet; el ah-shet; eel zah-shet; el zah-shet; noo zahsh-tong; voo zahsh-tay.

Exercise 15

Tell your friend …

1 … to reserve two rooms.
2 … to look for François.
3 … to seize the opportunity.
4 … to choose the Hugo method.
5 … to take up the luggage.

Tell your friend ...

6 ... not to eat too much.
7 ... not to put on weight.
8 ... not to smoke.

And now make some suggestions:

9 Let's speak French.
10 Let's listen to the radio.
11 Let's finish the report.

Vocabulary

le régime	diet
la gymnastique	gymnastics, exercises
la chose	thing
la vie	life
penser	to think
je pense que	I think that
je dois	I must
faire	to do
(vous faites)	
raccourcir	to shorten
chaque	each
certain	certain
bien	good, fine *(as adverb)*
complètement	completely
régulièrement	regularly
toujours	always
entre	for, between
pour	in order to
bonjour	good morning, good afternoon

IMITATED PRONUNCIATION: ray-zheem; zheem-nah-steek; shohz; vee; pah*ng*-say; zher pah*ng*s ker; zher dwah; fairr; voo fet; rah-koor-seerr; shahk; sairr-ta*ng*; bee-ang; ko*ng*-plet-mah*ng*; ray-gül-yairr-mah*ng*; too-zhoorr; ah*ng*tr; poorr; bo*ng*-zhoorr.

CONVERSATION

Un dialogue entre un homme d'affaires et une diététicienne.

Homme d'affaires	Bonjour, Madame.
Diététicienne	Bonjour, Monsieur. Un petit instant, s'il vous plaît, je finis ce rapport. Bon. Comment allez-vous?
Homme d'affaires	Je pense que je grossis.
Diététicienne	Ah? Vous ne réussissez pas à maigrir? Pourquoi pas?
Homme d'affaires	J'ai toujours faim. J'ai toujours soif. Qu'est-ce que je dois faire?
Diététicienne	Faites votre gymnastique régulièrement. Saisissez chaque occasion pour manger de la salade.
Homme d'affaires	Et qu'est-ce que je ne dois pas faire?
Diététicienne	Ne choisissez jamais de gâteaux. Ne choisissez jamais de glaces. Ne choisissez jamais de fromage.
Homme d'affaires	Très bien. Et pour le vin?
Diététicienne	Ne remplissez jamais votre verre complètement.
Homme d'affaires	Vous garantissez ce régime, Madame?
Diététicienne	Oui. Une chose est certaine: si vous grossissez, vous raccourcissez votre vie.
Homme d'affaires	Oui, Madame, vous avez raison.

TRANSLATION

A dialogue between a businessman and a dietitian.

Businessman	Good morning (madam).
Dietitian	Good morning (sir). One moment, please, I'll just finish (*literally* I finish) this report. Good. How are you?
Businessman	I think that I'm putting on weight.
Dietitian	Oh? You're not managing to lose weight? Why not?
Businessman	I'm always hungry. I'm always thirsty. What must I do?
Dietitian	Do your exercises regularly. Seize every opportunity to eat salad.
Businessman	And what must I not do?
Dietitian	Never choose cakes. Never choose ice cream. Never choose cheese.
Businessman	Fine. And what about wine?
Dietitian	Never fill your glass completely.
Businessman	Do you guarantee this diet (madam)?
Dietitian	Yes. One thing is certain: if you put on weight, you shorten your life.
Businessman	Yes (Madam). You're right.

Chapter 4

Chapter 4 introduces you to the perfect tense (enabling you to talk about the past), in both its affirmative and negative forms. You will also learn about:

- *possessive adjectives ("my," "your," "his," etc.)*
- *expressing the time*
- *an important irregular verb, "**partir**" ("to leave")*
- *more numbers*
- *seasons, months, dates, and days of the week*
- *the position of adjectives (before/after the noun)*

17 The perfect tense

You will often wish to talk about things that you have done. The French perfect tense translates all three forms of the English past: "I have spoken," "I did speak," "I spoke."

To form the perfect tense we:
a) change the **-er** of the infinitive into **-é**
b) change the **-ir** of the infinitive into **-i**

Verbs ending in **-er**	Verbs ending in **-ir**
j'ai parle	j'ai fini
tu as prepare	tu as garanti
il a habité	il a choisi
elle a travaillé	elle a grossi
nous avons regardé	nous avons maigri
vous avez écouté	vous avez saisi
ils ont voyagé	ils ont raccourci
elles ont téléphoné	elles ont rempli

Vocabulary

le document	document
l'Italie (*f.*)	Italy
la Manche	English Channel
copier	to copy
dépenser	to spend (money)
passer	to spend (time)
traverser	to cross

IMITATED PRONUNCIATION (17): pahr-lay; pray-pah-ray; ah-bee-tay; etc., fee-nee; gah-rah*ng*-tee; shwah-zee; etc., do-kü-mah*ng*; ee-tah-lee; mah*ng*sh; kop-yay; day-pah*ng*-say; pah-say; trah-vairr-say.

Exercise 16

Translate:

1 I have lived in France.
2 I have worked in Italy.
3 I have reserved the rooms.
4 She listened to the radio.
5 She watched television.
6 She prepared the report.
7 He has put on weight.
8 He has chosen the cheese.
9 He has finished the book.
10 We copied the document.
11 We bought the car.
12 We called (on the phone).
13 You guaranteed the tape recorder.
14 You seized the opportunity.
15 You invited the President.
16 They *(m.)* have lost weight.
17 They *(f.)* have spent 15 francs.
18 They *(f.)* have crossed the English Channel.

18 The perfect tense (negative)

You will also wish to say what you have not done:

je n'ai pas copié
tu n'as pas traversé
il n'a pas passé
elle n'a pas acheté
nous n'avons pas invité
vous n'avez pas garanti
ils n'ont pas rempli
elles n'ont pas fini

Note the position of **pas**

Exercise 17

Answer the questions as follows:

Avez-vous travaillé en Italie? Have you worked in Italy?
Non, je n'ai pas travaillé en Italie. No, I have not worked
in Italy.

1 Avez-vous réservé la chambre?
2 Avez-vous écouté le disque?
3 A-t-il regardé le film?
4 A-t-elle préparé le document?
5 Est-ce que nous avons fini?
6 Est-ce qu'ils ont choisi?
7 Est-ce qu'elles ont mangé?

19 Possessive adjectives

It is important to be able to establish ownership:

	m.sing.	*f.sing.*	*m. & f. pl.*
my	**mon**	**ma**	**mes**
your *(fam.)*	**ton**	**ta**	**tes**
his/her/its	**son**	**sa**	**ses**
our	**notre**	**notre**	**nos**
your	**votre**	**votre**	**vos**
their	**leur**	**leur**	**leurs**

Note: these adjectives agree with the thing possessed,
not with the possessor:

ma femme	my wife
son mari	her husband
votre chambre	your bedroom
nos clés	our keys
leurs disques	their records

Note also that if a feminine noun begins with a vowel, we write **mon, ton, son,** not **ma, ta, sa**:

mon amie	my friend
ton agence	your agency
son enquête	his/her survey

This sounds more pleasant to the French ear.

Vocabulary

le vol	flight
l'horaire (*m.*)	timetable
la ceinture de sécurité	seat belt
la place	seat
attacher	to fasten, to attach
premier, première (*f.*)	first

IMITATED PRONUNCIATION (19): mong; mah; may; tong; tah; tay; song; sah; say; notr; noh; votr; voh; lerr; fahm; mah-ree; vol; o-rairr; sang-tür der say-kü-ree-tay; plahs; ah-tah-shay; prerm-yay; prerm-yairr.

Exercise 18

Translate:

1 Your first flight.
2 Fasten your seat belt.
3 Where are our tickets?
4 Here is her passport.
5 Here is his seat.
6 Their suitcases are in the plane.
7 Our timetable is important.
8 Where are my newspapers?

20 The expression c'est ("it is")

C'est facile. It is easy.
C'est difficile. It is difficult.
C'est très important. It is very important.
C'est moins cher. It is less expensive.

Vocabulary

possible	possible
impossible	impossible
magnifique	wonderful
affreux	awful
tôt	early
tard	late

IMITATED PRONUNCIATION: say; mwah*ng*; po-seebl; a*ng*-po-seebl; mahn-yee-feek; ah-fre*r*; toh; tahr.

Exercise 19

Give the opposite of:

1 C'est intéressant.
2 C'est bon.
3 C'est possible.
4 C'est facile.
5 C'est magnifique.
6 C'est tard.

21 Time

If you intend to keep appointments, catch trains and buses, etc., you must be familiar with the way in which the French express time:

Quelle heure est-il? What time is it?
Il est une heure. It is one o'clock.
Il est deux heures. It is two o'clock.
Il est trois heures. It is three o'clock.
Il est quatre heures. It is four o'clock.
Il est midi. It is noon.
Il est minuit. It is midnight.

Il est cinq heures et quart. It is a quarter after five.
Il est cinq heures et demie. It is 5:30.
Il est six heures moins le quart. It is a quarter to six.

Il est six heures dix. It is ten after six.
Il est sept heures moins cinq. It is five to seven.

À quelle heure? At what time?
À huit heures. At eight o'clock.

À neuf heures du matin. At nine in the morning.
À neuf heures du soir. At nine in the evening.
À deux heures de l'après-midi. At two in the afternoon.

Vocabulary

le car	bus
le bateau	boat
l'aéroglisseur (*m.*)	hovercraft
le président	president, chairman
la conférence de presse	press conference
arriver	to arrive

Irregular verb:

partir (to leave)

Present tense
je pars
tu pars
il/elle part
nous partons
vous partez
ils/elles partent

IMITATED PRONUNCIATION (21): kel e*rr* ay teel; eel ay ün e*rr*;
eel ay de*r* ze*rr*; trwah ze*rr*; mee-dee; meen-wee; kahr; de*r*-mee;
ah kel e*rr*; ah ne*r* ve*rr* dü mah-ta*ng*; dü swahr;
de*r* lah-pray-mee-dee; kahr; bah-toh; ah-ay-roh-glee-se*rr*;
pray-zee-dah*ng*; ko*ng*-fay-rah*ng*ss de*r* press; ah-ree-vay;
pahr-teerr; pahr; pahr-to*ng*; pahr-tay; pahrt.

Exercise 20

Add 15 minutes to the time stated:

1 Il est deux heures.
2 Il est quatre heures et quart.
3 Il est six heures moins le quart.
4 Il est huit heures cinq.
5 Le train arrive à dix heures.
6 Le car arrive à onze heures et demie.
7 Le bateau part à midi dix.
8 L'aéroglisseur part à minuit et demi*.
9 Le Président arrive à neuf heures.
10 La conférence de presse est à dix heures.

*Demi agrees with minuit (m.); write demie to agree with
heure (f.).

22 Numerals

Here are some more numbers:

16	seize	33	trente-trois
17	dix-sept	40	quarante
18	dix-huit	41	quarante et un
19	dix-neuf	42	quarante-deux
20	vingt	50	cinquante
21	vingt et un	51	cinquante et un
22	vingt-deux	52	cinquante-deux
23	vingt-trois	60	soixante
30	trente	61	soixante et un
31	trente et un	62	soixante-deux
32	trente-deux		

IMITATED PRONUNCIATION (22): sez; dee-set; deez-weet; deez-ne*r*f; va*ng*; va*ng*-tay-u*ng*; va*ng*t-de*r*; va*ng*t-trwah; trah*ng*t; kah-rah*ng*t; sa*ng*-kah*ng*t; swah-sah*ng*t.

23 Seasons of the year

le printemps	spring
l'été *(m.)*	summer
l'automne *(m.)*	fall
l'hiver *(m.)*	winter

The seasons are all masculine.

en été	in the summer
en automne	in the fall
en hiver	in the winter
but	
au printemps	in the spring

24 Months of the year

janvier	January
février	February
mars	March
avril	April
mai	May
juin	June
juillet	July
août	August
septembre	September
octobre	October
novembre	November
décembre	December

Note that the months of the year are not written with a capital letter in French.

IMITATED PRONUNCIATION (23/24): ler prang-tahng; lay-tay; loh-ton; lee-vairr; zhahngv-yay; fayvr-yay; mahrss; ah-vreel; may; zhwang; zhwee-yay; oo OR oot; sep-tahngbr; ok-tobr; no-vahngbr; day-sahngbr.

25 Dates

Quelle date sommes-nous aujourd'hui?
   What is the date today?
Nous sommes le deux janvier. It's January 2nd.
Nous sommes le huit février. It's February 8th.
Nous sommes le quinze mars. It's March 15th.
Nous sommes le vingt avril. It's April 20th.
Nous sommes le trente mai. It's May 30th.

Note: for the "first" of each month we use **le premier**:

le premier juin	June 1st
le premier juillet	July 1st

BUT

le vingt et un août	August 21st
le trente et un octobre etc.	October 31st

Note also:

en août	in August
en septembre	in September
en octobre	in October
en novembre etc.	in November

Exercise 21

Write out in full the following dates:

1 New Year's Day
2 St. Valentine's Day
3 the first day of spring
4 April Fools' Day
5 St. Patrick's Day
6 the Allied invasion of Normandy
7 the storming of the Bastille
8 Halloween
9 the first day of fall
10 the Russian Revolution
11 Independence Day
12 Christmas Day

26 Days of the week

lundi	Monday
mardi	Tuesday
mercredi	Wednesday
jeudi	Thursday
vendredi	Friday
samedi	Saturday
dimanche	Sunday

Note that the days of the week are not written with a capital letter in French.

Examples:
Avez-vous travaillé lundi? Did you work on Monday?
Pierre téléphone jeudi. Pierre is calling on Thursday.
Pierre téléphone le jeudi. Pierre calls on Thursdays.

Note: "on" is omitted in French. **Le** indicates that the action takes place regularly.

IMITATED PRONUNCIATION (25/26): daht; oh-zhoor-dwee; lung-dee; mahr-dee; mairr-krer-dee; zher-dee; vahng-drer-dee; sahm-dee; dee-mahngsh.

Exercise 22

Translate:

1 I worked on Monday.
2 I listened to the radio on Tuesday.
3 I watched television on Wednesday.
4 I finished the report on Thursday.
5 I bought a record on Friday.
6 I called my wife on Saturday.
7 I spoke Spanish on Sunday.
8 I work on Mondays.
9 She listens to the radio on Tuesdays.
10 We watch television on Wednesdays.

27 The position of adjectives

In French, adjectives are usually placed after the noun:

un livre difficile	a difficult book
un médecin français	a French doctor
une voiture américaine	an American car
une langue importante	an important language

The following adjectives normally precede the noun:

bon, bonne *(f.)*	good
mauvais	bad
petit	small
grand	large
joli	pretty
jeune	young
vieux *(m. sing. & pl.)*	old
vieil *(m. sing.* before a vowel or h)	
vieille *(f.)*	
vieilles *(f. pl.)*	
nouveau *(m. sing.)*	new
nouvel *(m. sing* before a vowel or h)	
nouvelle *(f.)*	
nouveaux *(m. pl.)*	
nouvelles *(f. pl.)*	

Examples:

un bon employé	a good employee
un jeune pilote	a young pilot
un vieil ordinateur	an old computer
un nouvel électrophone	a new record player
une mauvaise cliente	a bad client
une jolie secrétaire	a pretty secretary

IMITATED PRONUNCIATION (27): zho-lee; zhern; vyer; vyay'ee; noo-voh; noo-vel; ahng-plwah-yay; klee-yahngt; ser-kray-tairr.

Vocabulary

Londres *(m.)*	London
l'argent *(m.)*	money
le départ	departure
la conversation	conversation
la semaine	week
les vacances *(f.)*	vacations
la nourriture	food
la chaleur	heat
l'intention *(f.)*	intention
la nage	swimming
visiter	to visit
trouver	to find
consulter	to consult
il faut	one must
indigeste	indigestible
insupportable	unbearable
moi	me (*see Chapter 8*)
un peu	a little
à l'avance	in advance
des	of the (**de** + **les** = **des**)

IMITATED PRONUNCIATION: longdr; ahr-zhahng; day-pahr; kong-vairr-sah-see-ong; ser-men; vah-kahngss; noo-ree-türr; shah-lerr; ang-tahng-see-ong; nahzh; vee-zee-tay; troo-vay; kong-sül-tay; eel foh; ang-dee-zhest; ang-sü-porr-tahbl; mwah; ung per; ah lah-vahngss; day.

CONVERSATION

À une agence de voyages à Londres.

Une conversation entre un employé français et
une cliente américaine qui habite à Londres. La cliente
saisit l'occasion pour parler français.

Cliente	Mon mari et moi, nous désirons passer deux semaines en France au printemps. Nous avons visité l'Italie en août, mais nous n'avons pas passé de bonnes vacances.
Employé	Ah? Pourquoi pas?
Cliente	Nous avons trouvé la nourriture un peu indigeste, nous avons trouvé la chaleur
	insupportable et nous avons dépensé beaucoup d'argent.
Employé	Avez-vous l'intention de voyager en avion?
Cliente	Non, en voiture, c'est moins cher.
Employé	Un petit instant, Madame, je consulte l'horaire des aéroglisseurs. Il y a un départ à huit heures, à neuf heures, à dix heures, à onze heures, etc. Il faut réserver les places à l'avance.
Cliente	Oui, oui, oui. Je n'ai pas l'intention de traverser la Manche à la nage!

TRANSLATION

At a travel agency in London.

A conversation between a French clerk and an American client living in London. The client seizes the opportunity to speak French.

Client   My husband and I wish to spend two weeks in France in the spring. We visited Italy in August, but we didn't have a good vacation.

Clerk   Oh? Why not?

Client   We found the food a little indigestible, we found the heat unbearable, and we spent a lot of money.

Clerk   Do you intend to travel by plane?

Client   No, by car, it's less expensive.

Clerk   Just one moment, madam. I'll consult the hovercraft timetable. There's a departure at eight o'clock, at nine o'clock, at ten o'clock, at eleven o'clock, etc. One must reserve seats in advance.

Client   Yes, yes, yes. I don't intend to swim across (*literally* to cross at the swimming) the English Channel!

Self-Assessment Test 1

This Self-Assessment Test, based on Lessons 1-4, allows you to check on your progress and see whether any revision is needed. Deduct one point for every grammatical mistake or misspelling. The answers and score assessment are in the Key.

A: Nouns Total: 8 points

Give the French for:

1 the doctor
2 the computer
3 some wine
4 some beer

5 my car
6 my keys
7 this train
8 these newspapers

B: Adjectives Total: 5 points

Give the opposite of:

1 pauvre
2 malheureux
3 intéressant

4 magnifique
5 facile

C: Verbs Total: 10 points

Which French verb do you associate with the following?

1 la télévision
2 la radio
3 la méthode Hugo
4 un sport
5 une cigarette
6 une chambre d'hôtel
7 une agence de voyages
8 l'occasion pour parler français
9 l'horaire des trains
10 la Manche

D: The time   Total: 8 points

Add fifteen minutes to the time mentioned:

1 Le train part à six heures.
2 Le car part à huit heures et demie.
3 Le Premier ministre arrive à dix heures cinq.
4 La conférence de presse est à onze heures et demie.

E: Days of the week   Total: 4 points

Write down the day before the one shown:

1 jeudi
2 lundi
3 samedi
4 mercredi

F: Total: 4 points

*What difference in meaning is there between **jeudi** and **le jeudi**?*

G: Months of the year   Total: 4 points

Write down the month after the one shown:

1 le deux janvier
2 le cinq mars
3 le douze mai
4 le trente et un juillet

H: The perfect tense   Total: 8 points

It all happened on Monday! Answer these questions in the perfect past, as in this example:

Q- Avez-vous l'intention de regarder le film?
A- Non, j'ai regardé le film lundi.

1 Avez-vous l'intention de réserver les chambres?
2 A-t-il l'intention de finir le livre?
3 A-t-elle l'intention de copier le document?
4 Ont-ils l'intention de téléphoner?

I: The perfect tense (negative) Total: 16 points

Give the French for:

1 haven't finished the report.
2 She didn't call her husband on Saturday.
3 We haven't visited Italy.
4 They *(m.)* haven't lost weight.

J: Numerals Total: 18 points

Complete the following, writing the totals in words:

a) 14 + 15
b) 20 + 16
c) 23 + 22
d) 27 + 4
e) 14 + 30
f) 30 + 20
g) 10 + 5
h) 30 + 32
i) 14 + 2

K: Do you remember ... ? Total: 1 point

Which verb do the French use when talking about a person's age?

L: Conversation (Role-play) Total: 14 points

Play the part of the customer in this short scene:

Cliente: We want to spend two weeks in France in the spring. We visited Italy in August, but we found the heat unbearable.
Employé: Avez-vous l'intention de voyager en avion?
Cliente: No, by car, it's less expensive.
Employé: Un petit instant, Madame, je consulte l'horaire des aéroglisseurs. Il faut réserver les places à l'avance.

Chapter 5

This chapter introduces regular and irregular "-re" verbs, in both present and perfect tenses. Other topics include:

- *introduction to adverbs*
- *personal pronouns used as object pronouns (direct/indirect)*
- *how direct object pronouns must agree in the perfect tense*
- *more irregular verbs, including the perfect tenses of "être" and "avoir"*

28 Regular verbs ending in -re

A number of important verbs end in **-re**:

vendre	to sell
rendre	to give back
attendre	to wait (for)
entendre	to hear
descendre	to take/bring down
répondre	to reply
perdre	to lose

We form the present tense by removing the **-re** from the infinitive and adding:

je	-s	**nous**	-ons
tu	-s	**vous**	-ez
il/elle	- -	**il/elles**	-ent

68

je vends	I sell (or I am selling)
tu vends	
il/elle vend	
nous vendons	
vous vendez	
ils/elles vendent	

The perfect tense is formed by changing the **-re** of the infinitive into **-u**:

j'ai vendu	I sold (or I have sold)
tu as vendu	
il/elle a vendu	
nous avons vendu	
vous avez vendu	
ils/elles ont vendu	

Vocabulary

les parents *(m.)*	parents
le frère	brother
la musique	music
la maison	house
la mère	mother
cela	that
dépendre de	to depend on
défendre	to defend, to forbid

IMITATED PRONUNCIATION (28): vahngdr; rahngdr; ah-tahngdr; ahng-tahngdr; day-sahngdr; ray-pongdr; pairrdr; vahng; vahng-dong; vahng-day; vahngd; vahng-dü; pah-rahng; frairr; mü-zeek; may-zong; mairr; ser-lah; day-pahngdr der; day-fahngdr.

Exercise 23

Translate:

1 I am selling my car.
2 He is waiting for his wife.
3 We give back sixty francs.
4 That depends on my parents.
5 Do they *(f.)* hear the music?
6 She has sold her house.
7 We have not replied.
8 Have you brought down the luggage?
9 Are you *(fam. sing.)* waiting for your brother?
10 Have you *(fam. sing.)* lost your mother?

29 Irregular -re verbs

The following **-re** verbs are irregular, taking a slightly different pattern in the present tense and a very different pattern in the perfect tense:

prendre	to take	**comprendre**	to understand
apprendre	to learn	**surprendre**	to surprise

Present

je prends I take (or I am taking)
tu prends
il/elle prend
nous prenons
vous prenez
ils/elles prennent

Perfect

j'ai pris I took (or I have taken)
j'ai appris I learned
j'ai compris I understood
j'ai surpris I surprised

IMITATED PRONUNCIATION (29): prah*ng*dr; ah-prah*ng*dr;
ko*ng*-prah*ng*dr; sür-prah*ng*dr; prah*ng*; pre*r*-no*ng*; pre*r*-nay; pren;
pree; ah-pree; ko*ng*-pree; sür-pree.

Exercise 24

Change the present to the past and vice versa:

1 Est-ce que vous prenez le train?
2 J'apprends le français.
3 Avez-vous appris la langue?
4 Avez-vous compris?
5 Tu surprends souvent ton professeur?

---

30 Other irregular -re verbs

The following irregular -re verbs have a similar pattern to
that of the "prendre" group but the consonant is doubled in
the nous, vous, and ils/elles forms:

mettre	to put
permettre	to permit
promettre	to promise
soumettre	to submit

Present

je mets	I put (or I am putting)
tu mets	
il/elle met	
nous mettons	
vous mettez	
ils/elles mettent	

Perfect

vous avez mis	you put (or you have put)
vous avez permis	you permitted
vous avez promis	you have promised
vous avez soumis	you have submitted

Vocabulary

le matin	morning
le dictionnaire	dictionary
le projet	project, plan
l'enfant *(m. & f.)*	child
l'annonce *(f.)*	advertisement
la lettre	letter
permettre de	to allow to
promettre de	to promise to
rentrer	to return
tôt	early
tard	late
déjà	already

IMITATED PRONUNCIATION (30): metr; pairr-metr; pro-metr; soo-metr; may; met-*ong*; met-ay; met; mee; pairr-mee; pro-mee; soo-mee; mah-ta*ng*; deeks-yo-nairr; pro-zhay; ah*ng*-fah*ng*; ah-no*ng*s; letr; rah*ng*-tray; toh; tahr; day-zhah.

Note the construction with **défendre and permettre:**
Je défends à Paul de parler. I forbid Paul to speak.
Je permets à Paul de parler. I allow Paul to speak.

Exercise 25

Change the present to the past and vice versa:

1 Je mets une annonce dans le journal.
2 Il permet à sa secrétaire de partir tôt.
3 Vous promettez de répondre à la lettre?
4 Elle soumet le rapport ce matin.
5 Avez-vous mis le dictionnaire dans la valise?
6 Ont-ils permis à leurs enfants de rentrer tard?
7 Nous avons promis de parler français.
8 Avez-vous déjà soumis le projet?

31 Adverbs

We often need to describe *how* things are done, for example:
rapidly, admirably, carefully.

In French, adverbs are formed by adding **-ment** to the
adjective, which is the equivalent of **-ly** in English:

rapide (rapid) becomes **rapidement** (rapidly)
admirable becomes **admirablement**
rare becomes **rarement**

If the adjective ends in a consonant, such as **malheureux**
(unfortunate), **-ment** is added to the feminine form:

immédiat	**immédiate** *(f.)*	**immédiatement**
général	**générale** *(f.)*	**généralement**
malheureux	**malheureuse** *(f.)*	**malheureusement**

Vocabulary

attentif, attentive (f.)	careful
complet, complète (f.)	complete
lent	slow
normal	normal
principal	main
temporaire	temporary

IMITATED PRONUNCIATION (31): rah-peed; rah-peed-mah*ng*; ahd-mee-rahbl; ahd-mee-rah-bler-mah*ng*; rahr; rahr-mah*ng*; ee-mayd-yaht-mah*ng*; zhay-nay-rahl-mah*ng*; mah-ler-rerz-mah*ng*; ah-tah*ng*-teef; ah-tah*ng*-teev; ko*ng*-play; ko*ng*-plet; lah*ng*; norr-mahl; pra*ng*-see-pahl; tah*ng*-po-rairr.

Exercise 26

Form adverbs from the following adjectives:

1 rapide
2 facile
3 final
4 heureux
5 attentif
6 lent
7 complet
8 normal
9 principal
10 temporaire

32 The pronoun "it"

When "it" refers to something that has just been mentioned, we use the same word in French as for "he" or "she," depending on the gender of the noun:

Le vin? Il est très bon. The wine? It's very good.
La voiture? Elle est chère. The car? It's expensive.

Referring to things, "they" is expressed by **ils** or **elles**:
Les trains? Ils sont rapides.
 The trains? They're fast.
Les places? Elles sont réservées.
 The seats? They're reserved.

Vocabulary

l'appareil (*m.*)	machine
le restaurant	restaurant
le produit	product
le message	message
le répondeur automatique	answering machine
la poche	pocket
la qualité	quality
l'explication (*f.*)	explanation
clair	clear
en anglais	in English
excellent	excellent

IMITATED PRONUNCIATION: ah-pah-ray'ee; res-to-rah*ng*; pro-dwee; may-sahzh; ray-po*ng*-de*rr*; oh-toh-mah-teek; posh; kah-lee-tay; eks-plee-kah-see-o*ng*; klairr; ah*ng* nah*ng*-glay; ek-sel-ah*ng*.

Exercise 27

Translate:

1 The report? It's very important.
2 The beer? It's bad.
3 The pocket? It's full.
4 The machine? It's excellent.
5 The restaurant? It's closed.
6 The quality? It's very good.
7 The products? They're French.
8 The messages? They're in English.
9 The explanation? It's not clear.
10 The answering machine? It's not expensive.

33 Personal pronouns – direct and indirect object

Study the following:

Michel le rencontre Michel meets him
Michel la rencontre Michel meets her
Michel les rencontre Michel meets them
Hélène le vend *(masc. word)* Hélène sells it
Hélène la vend *(fem. word)* Hélène sells it
Paul nous félicite Paul congratulates us
Paul vous félicite Paul congratulates you
Sophie me choisit Sophie chooses me
Sophie te choisit *(fam. sing.)* Sophie chooses you
Sophie vous comprend *(fam. pl.)* Sophie understands you

You will have noticed that:

a) "me," "him," "her," "us," "them," etc., are placed *before* the verb in French

b) the words for "him," "her," "it," and "them" are just like the words for "the"

c) the words for "us" and "you" are just like those for "we" and "you" (subject)

d) "me" in French is **me**

e) "you," familiar singular, is **te**

f) "you," familiar plural, remains **vous**

Me, **nous**, **vous**, and **te** can also mean "to me," "to us," "to you":

il me parle	he speaks to me
il nous répète	he repeats to us
elle vous répond	she replies to you
elle te vend *(fam.)*	she sells to you

Both "to him" and "to her" are translated by **lui:**

je lui répète   I repeat to him (or to her)

We express "to them" by **leur:**

je leur parle   I speak to them

Sometimes the "to" is not expressed in English, although clearly intended. Compare the French and the English below:

Je lui vends la voiture. I sell him the car.
Nous leur téléphonons. We call them.

Note: **me, le, la,** and **te** become **m', l', t',** in front of a vowel or h: **il m'invite; elle l'écoute; je t'invite.**

Vocabulary

le client	client
le mode d'emploi	operating instructions
l'ami *(m.)*	friend
l'amie *(f.)*	friend
la leçon	lesson
la commerçante	storekeeper
brancher	to plug in
mettre en marche	to start, to get going

IMITATED PRONUNCIATION: klee-yah*ng*; mod dah*ng*-plwah; ah-mee; ah-mee; le*r*-so*ng*; ko-mairr-sah*ng*t; brah*ng*-shay; metr ah*ng* mahrsh.

Exercise 28

Answer the questions using pronouns, as follows:

Vous me comprenez? Do you understand me?
Oui, je vous comprends. Yes, I understand you.

1 Elle me cherche?
2 Elle vous consulte?
3 Vous rencontrez le client?
4 Vous copiez la leçon?
5 Il invite Nicole?
6 Il exporte les voitures?
7 Comprenons-nous le mode d'emploi?
8 Branchons-nous la radio?
9 Mettons-nous l'appareil en marche?
10 Copions-nous le document?
11 Elles nous répondent en français?
12 Ils téléphonent à Pierre?
13 Ils téléphonent à Nicole?
14 Ils téléphonent à Pierre et à Nicole?
15 Vous parlez à la commerçante?
16 Vous répondez à vos amis?
17 Vous défendez à vos enfants de rentrer tard?

34 Direct object pronouns – agreement when used with perfect tense

When you use the direct* object pronouns with the perfect tense, there must be agreement, just as if you were dealing with an adjective:

je l'ai invité I invited him
je l'ai invitée I invited her
je les ai invités I invited them (men or men and women)
je les ai invitées I invited them (women)

*NOT the indirect object pronouns, i.e. *"to me,"* *"to him,"* etc.

vous l'avez copié you copied it (le document)
vous l'avez copiée you copied it (la leçon)
vous les avez copiés you copied them (les documents)
vous les avez copiées you copied them (les leçons)
vous les avez copiés you copied them (les documents
    et les leçons)

il m'a trouvé he found me (man speaking)
il m'a trouvée he found me (woman speaking)
il nous a trouvés he found us (men speaking)
il nous a trouvées he found us (women speaking)
il nous a trouvés he found us (men and women speaking)

elle vous a consulté she consulted you (you, a *(m)* doctor)
elle vous a consultée she consulted you (you, a *(f)* doctor)
elle vous a consultés she consulted you (you, *(m)* doctors)
elle vous a consultées she consulted you (you, *(f)* doctors)
elle vous a consultés she consulted you (you,*(m/ f)* doctors)

The pronunciation of all these endings is the same, i.e. "ay."
However, when the past participle ends in a consonant, for
example, **compris**, the addition of the feminine ending "**e**"
or "**es**" results in this consonant being sounded:

je l'ai comprise   I understood her
                          zher lay ko*ng*-preez

je les ai apprises   I learned them (les leçons, for example)
                          zher lay zay ah-preez

Exercice 29

Answer the questions as follows:

Avez-vous rencontré le client? Did you meet the client?
Oui, je l'ai rencontré. Yes, I met him.

1 Avez-vous invité Pierre?
2 Avez-vous invité Nicole?
3 Avez-vous invité Pierre et Nicole?
4 A-t-il exporté les voitures?
5 A-t-elle consulté le médecin?
6 A-t-elle consulté la diététicienne?
7 A-t-elle consulté le médecin et la diététicienne?
8 Ont-ils branché la radio?
9 Ont-ils réservé les chambres?
10 Ont-ils perdu la clé?
11 Avons-nous compris le mode d'emploi?
12 Avons-nous compris la leçon?
13 Avons-nous compris les leçons?
14 Avons-nous compris les livres?
15 Avez-vous mis la cassette dans votre poche?

Vocabulary

l'appel téléphonique *(m.)*	telephone call
ici	here
tout	everything
même	even
depuis	since
peut-être	perhaps
il y a	ago
seul	single, only
utiliser	to use
aux (à + les = aux)	to the
répéter	to repeat (see section 81, Chapter 12 for how **répéter** slightly changes its spelling in the present tense)

Irregular verbs:

lire (to read)

Present tense

je lis	**nous lisons**
tu lis	**vous lisez**
il/elle lit	**ils/elles lisent**

Perfect tense

j'ai lu, etc.

faire (to do, to make)

Present tense

je fais	**nous faisons**
tu fais	**vous faites**
il/elle fait	**ils/elles font**

Perfect tense

j'ai fait, etc.

être (to be)	**avoir** (to have)
Perfect tense	*Perfect tense*
j'ai été, etc.	**j ai eu**, etc.

IMITATED PRONUNCIATION: ah-pel tay-lay-fo-neek; ee-see;
too; mem; der-pwee; per-tetr; eel yah; serl; ü-tee-lee-zay; oh;
ray-pay-tay; zher ray-pet; tü ray-pet; eel ray-pet;
noo ray-pay-tong; voo ray-pay-tay; eel ray-pet; leerr; zher lee;
tü lee; eel lee; noo lee-zong; voo lee-zay; eel leez; zhay lü; fairr;
zher fay; tü fay; eel fay; noo fer-zong; voo fet; eel fong; zhay fay;
etr; zhay ay-tay; ah-vwahr; zhay ü.

CONVERSATION

Une conversation entre une commerçante et un client.

Client	Bonjour, Madame. Il y a deux semaines vous m'avez vendu un répondeur automatique. Malheureusement, il ne répond pas aux appels téléphoniques de mes amis.
Commerçante	Je suis surprise d'apprendre cela, Monsieur. Nos répondeurs sont d'excellente qualité. Avez-vous lu le mode d'emploi?
Client	Oui, je l'ai lu très attentivement. Attendez, je l'ai ici dans ma poche. Mais, où est-il? Je l'ai peut-être perdu.
Commerçante	Ce n'est pas grave, Monsieur. Avez-vous branché l'appareil correctement? Avez-vous mis l'appareil en marche? Avez-vous compris les explications?
Client	Oui, j'ai tout compris et j'ai tout fait correctement. J'ai même défendu à mes enfants de l'utiliser.
Commerçante	Permettez-moi de vous répéter, Monsieur, que nos produits sont d'excellente qualité. Si vous n'avez pas eu un seul message depuis deux semaines, la seule explication possible, c'est que personne ne vous téléphone!

TRANSLATION

A conversation between a storekeeper and a customer.

Customer Good morning. Two weeks ago you sold me an answering machine. Unfortunately, it doesn't answer my friends' telephone calls.

Storekeeper I'm surprised to hear (learn) that, Sir. Our answering machines are excellent quality. Have you read the instruction booklet?

Customer Yes, I read it very carefully. One moment (wait), I have it here in my pocket. But, where is it? Perhaps I've lost it.

Storekeeper It doesn't matter, Sir. Did you plug the machine in correctly? Did you start the machine? Did you understand the instructions (explanations)?

Customer Yes, I understood everything and I did everything correctly. I have even forbidden my children to use it.

Storekeeper Allow me to repeat (to you), Sir, that our products are of excellent quality. If you haven't had a single message for two weeks, the only possible explanation is that no one calls you!

Chapter 6

The principal topic in Chapter 6 is the comparison of
adjectives and adverbs, including the superlative
("small/smaller/smallest," etc.) and irregular forms
("good/better/best," etc.). You'll also learn about:

- prepositions
- the expression "**il y a**" ("there is/are")
- verbs that form their past tense with "**être**"
- the expressions "**je voudrais**" and "**il faut**"
    ("I would like ...," "one must/has to")

35 Prepositions

Here are some useful French prepositions. Many of them are
used to indicate position:

dans	in
en	in/to
sur	on
sous	under
devant	in front of
derrière	behind
près de	near
à côté de	next to
en face de	opposite
à	at/to
de	of/from
pour	for
avec	with

sans	without
après	after
avant	before

We saw in previous chapters that the French do not say
"**à le**" or "**à les**" but **au** and **aux**; instead of "**de le**" and "**de les**," they say **du** and **des**.

Examples:

au musée	at/to the museum
à la boulangerie	at/to the bakery
aux magasins	at/to the stores
du bureau de poste	of/from the post office
de la pharmacie	of/from the drugstore
des hôtels	of/from the hotels
dans la voiture	in the car
en France	in/to France
à côté de la boucherie	next to the butcher's
en face de la poissonnerie	opposite the fish market
près de l'épicerie	near the grocer's
sur la table	on the table
sous la chaise	under the chair
devant l'hôpital	in front of the hospital
derrière l'université	behind the university
avec mon mari	with my husband
sans difficulté	without difficulty
après le petit déjeuner	after breakfast
avant le dîner	before dinner

Note: both **dans** and **en** mean "in," but **dans** is more specific; i.e. **dans** is generally used before **le, la, les, un, une, mon, votre,** etc.; otherwise **en** is used. Contrast:

dans la voiture de mon frère	in my brother's car
en voiture	by (in) car
dans le sudde la France	in the south of France
en France	in France

Note also the following difference:

dans deux semaines	in two weeks' time
(I'll begin the work **"dans deux semaines"**)	

en deux semaines	within two weeks
(I did the work **"en deux semaines"**)	

36 The expression "il y a"

We have already met **il y a,** but let us look at this very useful expression more closely. It means "there is" or "there are" and can, therefore, be used with both singular and plural nouns:

Il y a un taxi devant l'hôtel.
> There's a taxi in front of the hotel.
Il y a des journaux ici.
> There are some newspapers here.
Est-ce qu'il y a une banque ici?
> Is there a bank here?

Vocabulary

le restaurant	restaurant
le supermarché	supermarket
le tunnel	tunnel
le numéro de téléphone	telephone number
le cinéma	movie theater
le théâtre	theater
le spectacle	show
l'ami *(m.)*	friend
les États-Unis	United States
la serviette	briefcase, towel, napkin
l'église *(f.)*	church
la librairie	bookstore
la bibliothèque	library
la cabine téléphonique	telephone booth
l'amie *(f.)*	friend
c'est difficile de	it is difficult to

Irregular verbs:

aller (to go)

Present tense

je vais
tu vas
il/elle va
nous allons
vous allez
ils/elles vont

venir (to come)

Present tense

je viens
tu viens
il/elle vient
nous venons vous venez
ils/elles viennent

IMITATED PRONUNCIATION: We feel that you should now be fairly confident as far as the pronunciation is concerned. Therefore we are discontinuing the imitated pronunciation at this point. If you are still having difficulty with this aspect of the language, and it has to be admitted that French pronunciation does present problems, we strongly recommend that you buy the cassette recordings that accompany this course.

Exercise 30

Translate:

1 There's a briefcase on the table.
2 There's a taxi in front of the hotel.
3 There's a restaurant behind the church.
4 There's a supermarket next to the bank.
5 There's a bookstore opposite the university.
6 Is there a telephone booth near the station?
7 Are there any American books in the library?
8 Is there a tunnel under the English Channel?
9 I'm going to the movies.
10 She's going to the United States.
11 Do you have the telephone number of the theater?
12 I have bought a newspaper for my friend.
13 She's learning French with some cassettes.
14 It's difficult to work without my secretary.
15 Let's eat after the show.
16 Let's call before 9 o'clock.

37 Comparison of adjectives

In English we make comparisons by adding "er" to the adjective or by using "more" or "less;" in French we simply put **plus** (more) and **moins** (less) in front of the adjective:

Cet hôtel est grand.
    This hotel is large.
Cet hôtel est plus grand.
    This hotel is larger.
Cette lettre est importante.
    This letter is important.
Cette lettre est plus importante.
    This letter is more important.
Ce livre est moins difficile.
    This book is less difficult.

We express "than" by **que:**

La cathédrale est plus belle que l'église.
    The cathedral is more beautiful than the church.
Le film est moins intéressant que le livre.
    The film is less interesting than the book.

Note also:

aussi ... que   as ... as
pas si ... que   not so ... as

L'aéroglisseur est aussi rapide que le tunnel sous la Manche.
    The hovercraft is as fast as the English Channel tunnel.
Le train n'est pas si rapide que l'avion.
    The train is not as fast as the plane.

38 Comparison of adverbs

Adverbs follow the same pattern as adjectives:

Pierre travaille lentement.
Pierre works slowly.
Paul travaille plus lentement que Pierre.
Paul works more slowly than Pierre.

Vocabulary

le banquier	banker
le facteur	mailman
le télégramme	telegram
le russe	Russian language
l'actrice	actress
courageux	brave
distinct	distinct
beau *(m.)*	beautiful

    bel *(m.)* before a vowel or h
    beaux *(m. pl.)*
    belle *(f.)*
    belles *(f. pl.)*

Exercise 31

Translate:

1 The banker is richer than the teacher.
2 The mailman is poorer than the lawyer.
3 The flight attendant is more beautiful than the actress.
4 The letter is less important than the telegram.
5 The pilot is as brave as the astronaut.
6 French is not as difficult as Russian (say *the* French ...
  the Russian).
7 She speaks more distinctly than Paul.
8 He listens more attentively than his brother.

N.B. We have seen that "than" is translated by **que.** However, when "than" is followed by a number, we use **de** in place of **que:**

J'ai plus de 40 francs. I have more than 40 francs.

39 Superlative of adjectives

In English, we form the superlative by adding "est" to the adjective or by using "most;" in French, we use **le plus, la plus,** or **les plus:**

Pierre est le plus petit de la classe.
　　Pierre is the smallest in the class.
Annette est la plus grande de la famille.
　　Annette is the tallest in the family.
Pierre et Nicole sont les plus intelligents du groupe.
　　Pierre and Nicole are the most intelligent in the group.
Michel est le plus jeune pilote de la compagnie aérienne.
　　Michel is the youngest pilot in the airline company.

You will have noticed that "in" is translated de after a superlative.

If the adjective is one that normally follows the noun, **le/la/les** are placed both before and after the noun:

le vin le plus cher the most expensive wine
les livres les plus intéressants the most interesting books

40 Superlative of adverbs

We put **le plus** in front of the adverb, irrespective of the gender of the subject:

Annette travaille le plus rapidement de tous.
　　Annette works the fastest of all.

41 Irregular comparisons of adjectives and adverbs

bon (good) → **meilleur** (better) → **le meilleur** (the best)
bonne → **meilleure** → **la meilleure** (*f.*)

mauvais (bad) → **pire** (worse) → **le pire** (the worst)

Note that **plus mauvais** and **le plus mauvais** are also possible and, in fact, are more usual.

bien (well) → **mieux** (better) → **le mieux** (the best)
peu (little) → **moins** (less) → **le moins** (the least)
beaucoup (much) → **plus** (more) → **le plus** (the most)

Examples:

Un bon restaurant.	A good restaurant.
Un meilleur restaurant.	A better restaurant.
Le meilleur restaurant.	The best restaurant.
Je chante bien.	I sing well.
Vous chantez mieux.	You sing better.
Il chante le mieux de tous.	He sings the best of all.

Vocabulary

le parc	park
le monde	world
la ville	town
chic	stylish
célèbre	famous
agréable	pleasant
confortable	comfortable
impressionnant	impressive

Exercise 32

You're showing a French friend around Texas. Try to convince him/her that "American is best" by replying to your friend's comments like this:

Ce parc est grand. This park is large.
Oui, c'est le plus grand parc du monde. Yes, this is the largest park in the world.

1 Ce restaurant est chic.
2 Cette librairie est grande.
3 Ce magasin est célèbre.
4 Cette cathédrale est belle.
5 Cette bière est bonne.
6 Ce parc est agréable.
7 Dallas est une ville intéressante.
8 La Cadillac est une voiture confortable.
9 Le "747" est un avion impressionnant.

42 The weather

The French often discuss the weather. The verb **faire** appears in many expressions connected with this topic:

Il fait beau. The weather is fine.
Il fait mauvais. The weather is bad.
Il fait chaud. It's hot.
Il fait froid. It's cold.
Il fait du vent. It's windy.
Il fait du soleil. It's sunny.
Il fait du brouillard. It's foggy.
Il pleut. It's raining.
Il neige. It's snowing.

Exercise 33

Which French expression describes the weather in the following situations?

1 An umbrella would be useful.
2 Due to poor visibility, there could be some traffic accidents.
3 Hold on to your hat!
4 You'll need a warm coat.
5 Dark glasses would be a great help.
6 It's nice when this happens at Christmas.
7 Open the window and let in a little cool air.
8 Probably best to stay at home.
9 A walk through the park would be nice.

43 Verbs conjugated with "être" (to be)

We saw in Chapter 4 that the past tense of most French verbs is formed with avoir (to have):

j'ai téléphoné	I called
vous avez fini	you finished

But some verbs, often denoting motion, form their past with **être.** The following verbs, some of which are irregular, are the most important:

aller *(irreg.)*	to go
arriver	to arrive
retourner	to return
monter	to go up to
rester	to stay
partir *(irreg.)*	to leave
sortir *(irreg.)*	to go out
venir *(irreg.)*	to come
revenir *(irreg.)*	to come back
descendre	to go down

Note: when **monter** and **descendre** mean, respectively, "to take up" and "to bring down," they are conjugated with **avoir** (see Exercise 23).

Examples:

je suis allé	I went
je suis arrivé	I arrived
il est parti	he left
il est sorti	he went out
vous êtes venu	you came
vous êtes descendu	you went down

The past participle (**allé, parti, venu,** etc.) of these verbs agrees in gender and number with the subject, just as if it were an adjective:

masc. sing.	*fem. sing.*
je suis allé	**je suis partie**
il est arrivé	**elle est sortie**
vous êtes retourné	**vous êtes venue**
tu es resté	**tu es descendue**

masc. pl.	*fem. pl.*
nous sommes allés	**nous sommes restées**
vous êtes partis	**vous êtes sorties**
ils sont revenus	**elles sont descendues**

Vocabulary

le bureau	office
l'étudiant *(m.)*	student
la réunion	meeting
la journée	day (daytime)
la maison	house, home
l'infirmière *(f.)*	nurse
l'étudiante *(f.)*	student
tout *(m.)*	all
tous *(m. pl.)*	
toute *(f.)*	
toutes *(f. pl.)*	

Exercise 34

A. Imagine for a moment the following:

You are a doctor (male). You arrived at the hospital this morning at seven o'clock. You went to a meeting at ten o'clock. You left the hospital with two nurses.

Now complete these sentences:

1 Je suis (doctor).
2 Ce matin je (arriver) à l'hôpital à 7 heures.
3 Je (aller) à une réunion à 10 heures.
4 Je (partir) avec deux infirmières.

B. Imagine the following:

You are a journalist (female). Yesterday, you went to a press conference. At one o'clock you went upstairs to the restaurant. You returned to the office very late.

Now complete these sentences:

1 Je suis (journalist).
2 Hier je (aller) à une conférence de presse.
3 Je (monter) au restaurant à une heure.
4 Je (retourner) au bureau très tard.

C. Consider the following:

Nicole and Sophie are students. They went to the university this morning at nine o'clock. They stayed in the library the whole day. They came back home at five o'clock.

Now complete these sentences:

1 Nicole et Sophie sont (students).
2 Ce matin elles (aller) à l'université à 9 heures.
3 Elles (rester) toute la journée à la bibliothèque.
4 Elles (revenir) à la maison à 5 heures.

Vocabulary

l'ingénieur *(m.)*	engineer
hier	yesterday
déjà	already
tôt	early

Exercise 35

Translate:

1 The engineers arrived yesterday.
2 The actresses have already left.
3 We *(f.)* came back early.
4 You *(fam. sing. m.)* went downstairs.
5 Did the nurse stay all day?
6 Did you come back very late?

44 The expression "je voudrais"

You will want to ask for things and to say what you would like to do. Use **je voudrais** (I would like):

Je voudrais un café.
   I would like coffee.
Je voudrais de la confiture.
   I would like some jam.
Je voudrais prendre le petit déjeuner dans ma chambre.
   I would like to have (take) breakfast in my room.
Je voudrais rester deux jours.
   I would like to stay two days.

Note:

a) if you ask for **café,** you will receive black coffee; if you want coffee with milk, ask for **un café crème** or, at break fast time, **un café au lait.**

b) **voudrais** is actually the conditional tense, which we will be studying later.

Vocabulary

le timbre	stamp
le plan	street map
le lait	milk
le sucre	sugar
le thé	tea
la carte postale	postcard
la note	bill (in a hotel)
l'addition (f.)	check (in a restaurant)
régler	settle

Irregular verb:

envoyer (to send)

Present tense

j'envoie
tu envoies
il/elle envoie
nous envoyons
vous envoyez
ils/elles envoient

Exercise 36

Ask for the following, using je voudrais:

1 a postcard
2 a stamp
3 a street map of the town
4 an American newspaper
5 some milk
6 some sugar
7 some tea

And now, say that you would like:

8 to call New York
9 to send a telegram
10 to settle the hotel bill

---

45 The expression "il faut"

If you want to say that something has to be done, you can use **il faut** (one must, it is necessary):

Il faut conduire à droite. One has to drive on the right.
Il faut aller à la pharmacie. One has to go to the drugstore.

Used with the indirect object pronoun, **il faut** means "need":

Il nous faut un dictionnaire. We need a dictionary.
Il lui faut 50 francs. He (or she) needs 50 francs.

Vocabulary

le crayon	pencil
le stylo-bille	ballpoint pen
le papier à lettres	writing paper
la gomme	eraser
l'enveloppe (f.)	envelope
l'allumette (f.)	match

Exercise 37

Say you need the following:

1 a pencil
2 a ballpoint pen

Now, she needs:

3 an eraser
4 some writing paper

Now, they need:

5 some envelopes
6 some cigarettes
7 some matches

Vocabulary

le port	port
le pain	bread
l'article *(m.)*	item
la place	square
la rue	street
la marque	brand
la promotion	special offer
la porte	door
l'année *(f.)*	year
tourner	to turn
recommander	to recommend
avoir le pied marin	to be a good sailor
tout droit	straight on
à gauche	on/to the left
à droite	on/to the right
d'habitude	usually
au revoir	good-bye
si	so
voilà	there is (pointing)
autre	other
rouge	red
quelques	a few
dernier, dernière *(f.)*	last

CONVERSATION

Un touriste américain passe la journée à Boulogne.

Touriste	Pardon, Madame. Je cherche une bonne épicerie, ici près du port.
Passante	La meilleure épicerie de Boulogne est sur la place, en face de la banque. Vous allez tout droit et vous prenez la première rue à gauche.
Touriste	Merci, Madame. (Il répète) … je vais tout droit, je tourne à droite … non, non … je tourne à gauche. Ah, voilà l'épicerie.

A l'épicerie

Épicière	Bonjour, Monsieur. Vous désirez?
Touriste	Bonjour, Madame. Je voudrais du fromage, du vin et de la bière, s'il vous plaît.
Épicière	Voici le fromage. C'est la meilleure marque. Il est plus cher que les autres fromages, mais il est excellent. Je vous recommande aussi ce vin rouge. Il est moins cher que d'habitude; il est en promotion.
Touriste	Bien. Je prends ces trois articles. Merci. Est-ce que vous vendez aussi du pain?
Épicière	Non, Monsieur. Pour cela, il faut aller à la boulangerie. La boulangerie est à côté du bureau de poste.
Touriste	Merci. Au revoir, Madame. (Il va à la porte) … Oh, il pleut! Et il fait du vent.
Épicière	Attendez quelques instants. Ici à Boulogne il fait rarement beau. Il pleut souvent et il fait toujours du vent.

Touriste   Oui. L'année dernière ma femme et moi,
nous sommes venus passer la journée ici,
mais il a fait si mauvais. Nous avons
attendu … je n'ai pas le pied marin.
Nous avons attendu un jour, deux jours.
Finalement, nous sommes restés une
semaine à Boulogne!

TRANSLATION

An American tourist spends the day in Boulogne.

Tourist   Excuse me. I'm looking for a good grocer,
here near the port.

Passerby   The best grocer's in Boulogne is in (on) the
square, opposite the bank. You go straight
ahead and you take the first street on the left.

Tourist   Thank you. (He repeats) … I go straight
ahead, I turn to the right … no, no … I turn
to the left. Ah, there's the grocer's.

At the grocer's

Grocer   Good morning, Sir. What would you like?
(*lit.* "you wish?")

Tourist   Good morning. I'd like some cheese, some
wine, and some beer, please.

Grocer   Here's the cheese. It's the best brand. It's
more expensive than the other cheeses, but
it's excellent. I also recommend (to you) this
red wine. It's less expensive than usual; it's
a special offer (*lit.* "in promotion.")

Tourist	Fine. I'll take (*lit.* "I take") these three items. Thank you. Do you sell bread?
Grocer	No, sir. For that, one has to go to the bakery. The bakery is next to the post office.
Tourist	Thank you. (*He goes to the door*) ... Oh, it's raining. And it's windy.
Grocer	Wait a few moments. Here in Boulogne the weather is rarely fine. It often rains and it's always windy.
Tourist	Yes. Last year my wife and I came to spend the day here, but the weather was so bad. We waited ... I'm not a good sailor (*lit.* "I don't have the sea foot"). We waited one day, two days. Finally, we spent a week in Boulogne!

Chapter 7

Now you'll learn how to use adverbs of quality, and the future tense (including some key verbs' irregular forms), and be introduced to the all-important modal verbs *"pouvoir,"* *"devoir," "vouloir,"* and *"savoir."* Other topics include:

- countries
- more numbers (up to 100)
- four more irregular verbs

46 Adverbs of quantity

Occasionally, you will need to talk about quantities. You may have too much of something or too little or not enough, etc.

Study the following:

beaucoup	much, many
trop	too much, too many
tant	so much, so many
peu	little, few
assez	enough

When a noun follows these words, they are linked by **de (d')**:

beaucoup de temps (*m.*)	much time
beaucoup de légumes (*m.*)	many vegetables
trop d'argent	too much money

trop de vêtements *(m.)*	too many clothes
peu de patience *(f.)*	little patience
assez de fruits *(m. pl.)*	enough fruit

The following are also linked to the noun by **de** (**d'**):

plus	more
moins	less, fewer
autant	as much, as many

Examples:

J'ai l'intention de boire plus d'eau.
    I intend to drink more water.
J'ai l'intention de manger moins de pain.
    I intend to eat less bread .
Rémi a autant de disques que Marie-Claude.
    Rémi has as many records as Marie-Claude.

Vocabulary

le mouchoir	handkerchief
le chapeau	hat
le pantalon	pair of pants
le foulard	scarf
le cardigan	cardigan, sweater
le costume	suit
la chemise	shirt
la cravate	tie
la robe	dress
la jupe	skirt
la chemise de nuit	nightgown

Exercise 38

Answer the questions.

Example:
Vous faut-il une chemise? Do you need a shirt?
Non, j'ai beaucoup de chemises. No, I have many shirts.

  1 Vous faut-il une cravate?
  2 Vous faut-il un mouchoir?
  3 Vous faut-il une robe?

Example:
Michel a acheté un chapeau? Has Michel bought a hat?
Oui, il a maintenant trop de chapeaux. Yes, he has too many hats now.

  4 Bernard a acheté un pantalon?
  5 Hélène a acheté une jupe?
  6 Marie-José a acheté un foulard?

Translate:

  7 He has little patience.
  8 Have you put enough nightgowns in the suitcase?
  9 I have more cardigans than Monique.
10 You have fewer suits than Pierre.

47 The future tense

You will often want to talk about what you plan to do in the future. There are three ways of doing this:

1 In conversation, you can often use the present tense with a future meaning:

Un petit instant, je finis ce rapport.
> One moment, I'll just finish this report. (See Chapter 3)

Bien. Je prends ces trois articles.
> Fine. I'll take these three items. (See Chapter 6)

J'arrive lundi.
> I'll arrive on Monday.

2 You can do what we do in English; i.e., use "to go," followed by another verb:

Je vais téléphoner demain.
> I'm going to call tomorrow.

Aujourd'hui il va manger dans un restaurant chic.
> Today he's going to eat in a stylish restaurant.

Nous allons regarder la télévision ce soir.
> We're going to watch television this evening.

3 You can use the future tense, which is formed by adding the following endings to the infinitive of the verb:

je	- ai
tu	- as
il/elle	- a
nous	- ons
vous	- ez
ils/elles	- ont

Examples:

je consulterai	I will consult
tu chanteras	you *(fam.)* will sing
il fumera	he will smoke
elle exportera	she will export
nous choisirons	we will choose
vous finirez	you will finish
ils garantiront	they will guarantee
elles réussiront	they *(f.)* will succeed

To form the future of **-re** verbs, drop the final **e** of the infinitive before adding the endings:

j'attendrai	I will wait
il apprendra	he will learn
nous comprendrons	we will understand
vous mettrez	you will put
ils promettront	they will promise

Some important verbs have an irregular future and we should learn them now:

avoir	j'aurai	I will have
être	je serai	I will be
aller	j'irai	I will go
faire	je ferai	I will do, make
venir	je viendrai	I will come
envoyer	j'enverrai	I will send
il y a	il y aura	there will be
il faut	il faudra	it will be necessary

Vocabulary

le tennis	tennis
le week-end	weekend
le père	father
l'appartement (*m.*)	apartment
la réunion	meeting
la conférence	conference
la mère	mother
les courses (*f.*)	shopping
international	international
étudier	to study
réparer	to repair
jouer	to play
visiter	to visit
tapisser	to wallpaper
organiser	to organize

Irregular verb:

écrire (to write)

Present tense

j'écris
tu écris
il/elle écrit
nous écrivons
vous écrivez
ils/elles écrivent

Perfect tense

j'ai écrit, etc.

Exercise 39

*Here is a list of things you plan to do tomorrow (**demain**). Translate the list into French, using the construction with **aller**. Write complete sentences.*

1 Listen to radio
2 Buy newspaper
3 Study French
4 Do shopping

*Here is Michel's list for next week (**la semaine prochaine**). Translate, using the future tense in complete sentences:*

5 Repair car
6 Play tennis
7 Write letter
8 Visit museum

*Here is Pierre and Hélène's list for next month (**le mois prochain**). Use the future tense and write complete sentences:*

9 Wallpaper apartment
10 Organize meeting
11 Go to international conference
12 Spend weekend in London

Translate:

13 She will finish her letter.
14 We will go to the theater next week.
15 You will surprise your father.
16 You *(fam.)* will choose your dress next month.

48 Modal verbs

These are auxiliary verbs that are used in conjunction with the infinitive of a following verb – for example, "I can come" or "We must telephone." There are four important modal verbs in French:

pouvoir   to be able to
devoir   to have to
vouloir   to want to
savoir   to know (how to)

1 Pouvoir
Sometimes you will want to talk about what you can or cannot do. Use the irregular verb **pouvoir:**

Present tense: I can

je peux
tu peux
il/elle peut
nous pouvons
vous pouvez
ils/elles peuvent

Past tense (perfect): **j'ai pu**, I was able to

Future tense: **je pourrai**, I will be able to

Examples:

Je peux faire les courses maintenant.
    I can do the shopping now.
Pouvez-vous me dire où est la gare?
    Can you tell me where the station is?
Avez-vous pu téléphoner à Paris ?
    Have you been able to call Paris?

In formal situations **puis-je** is sometimes used in place of **est-ce que je peux** to express "can I ...?" or "may I ...?"

2 Devoir

You will also want to talk about what you must or have to do. Use the irregular verb **devoir:**

Present tense: I must

je dois
tu dois
il/elle doit
nous devons
vous devez
ils/elles doivent

Past tense (perfect): **j'ai dû,** I had to

Future tense: **je devrai,** I will have to

Examples:

Je dois changer ma vie.
   I must change my life.
Vous devez envoyer une carte postale à votre ami.
   You must send a postcard to your friend.
Il a dû partir.
   He had to leave.
Elle devra apprendre l'espagnol.
   She will have to learn Spanish.

3 Vouloir

You have already met **je voudrais,** meaning "I would like;" this comes from the irregular verb **vouloir** (to want):

Present tense: I want

je veux
tu veux
il/elle veut
nous voulons
vous voulez
ils/elles veulent

Past tense (perfect): **j'ai voulu,** I wanted

Future tense: **je voudrai,** I will want

112

Examples:

Je veux changer mon argent américain en francs.
I want to change my American money into francs.
Nous voulons une chambre pour deux personnes.
We want a double room.

A request can be made more polite by putting **"Voulez-vous
…"** at the beginning of the sentence: **Voulez-vous signer ici?**
(Will you sign here?)

4 Savoir
The irregular verb **savoir** means "to know":

Present tense: I know

**je sais
tu sais
il/elle sait
nous savons
vous savez
ils/elles savent**

Past tense (perfect): **j'ai su**, I knew

Future tense: **je saurai**, I will know

Examples:

Je sais que vous voyagez à l'étranger.
I know that you travel abroad.
Savez-vous où je peux louer une voiture?
Do you know where I can rent a car?
Pierre saura demain s'il va être en chômage.
Pierre will know tomorrow if he's going to be
unemployed (lit. "in unemployment").

Savoir can also mean "to know how to":

Je sais jouer du piano.
I can (know how to) play the piano.

Note the difference between **pouvoir** and **savoir:**

Je ne sais pas jouer du piano.
> I can't play the piano. (I don't know how to)

Je ne peux pas jouer du piano.
> I can't play the piano. (my hand is bandaged)

Vocabulary

le diplomate	diplomat
le marché	market
le contrat	contract
l'écriture *(f.)*	handwriting
arrêter	to stop
arrêter de fumer	to stop smoking
décourager	to discourage
nager	to swim
garer	to park
faire le tour du monde	to tour the world

Irregular verb:

conduire (to drive)

Present tense

je conduis
tu conduis
il/elle conduit
nous conduisons
vous conduisez
ils/elles conduisent

Perfect tense

j'ai conduit, etc.

Exercise 40

Say that you can:

1 buy the vegetables at the market
2 prepare the report

Say that we cannot:

3 arrive on Monday
4 read his handwriting

Say that she must:

5 sign the contract
6 stop smoking

Say that they must not:

7 discourage the students
8 park the car in front of the hospital

Say that he wants to:

9 tour the world
10 spend less money

Ask your friend whether he/she knows how to:

11 drive
12 swim

49 Countries

In French, countries can be either masculine or feminine:

la Finlande	Finland
la Suède	Sweden
la France	France
la Belgique	Belgium
la Grande-Bretagne	Great Britain
la Grèce	Greece

la Hollande	Holland
la Chine	China
la Russie	Russia
l'Angleterre	England
l'Ecosse	Scotland
l'Allemagne	Germany
l'Italie	Italy
l'Espagne	Spain
l'Irlande	Ireland
l'Autriche	Austria
le Danemark	Denmark
le Portugal	Portugal
le Luxembourg	Luxemburg
le Canada	Canada
le Japon	Japan
le Pays de Galles	Wales
les États-Unis	United States
le Royaume-Uni	United Kingdom

Before a masculine country "in" or "to" is translated **au**:

au Pays de Galles	in/to Wales
au Portugal	in/to Portugal
au Japon	in/to Japan

Before a feminine country "in" or "to" is translated **en**:

en Angleterre	in/to England
en Écosse	in/to Scotland
en France	in/to France
en Chine	in/to China

We use **aux** for a country with a plural form:

aux États-Unis	in/to the United States

Exercise 41

Prepare a list of fifteen countries in Europe and indicate whether they are masculine or feminine.

Exercise 42

Translate:

1 We spend our vacations in Greece.
2 Do you intend to go to Japan?
3 Great Britain exports cars to France.
4 Has the diplomat arrived in Russia?

50 Numerals

Let's continue our study of the numbers:

63	soixante-trois	81	quatre-vingt-un
70	soixante-dix	82	quatre-vingt-deux
71	soixante et onze	88	quatre-vingt-huit
72	soixante-douze	90	quatre-vingt-dix
73	soixante-treize	91	quatre-vingt-onze
79	soixante-dix-neuf	99	quatre-vingt-dix-neuf
80	quatre-vingts	100	cent

Note that the **s** in **quatre-vingts** is omitted when another number follows.

Exercise 43

Complete the following, writing the answers in words:

a 10 + 10 =   g 40 + 30 =
b 10 + 12 =   h 19 + 60 =
c 11 + 20 =   i 40 + 41 =
d 27 + 20 =   j 41 + 50 =
e 30 + 29 =   k 19 + 80 =
f 21 + 40 =   l 50 + 50 =

Vocabulary

la résolution	resolution
la liste	list
la promesse	promise
la gymnastique	physical exercises
la santé	health
certain	certain
neuf, neuve *(f.)*	brand-new
quoi	what
quoi de neuf?	what's new?
eh bien?	well?
vraiment	really
ça = cela	that
souhaiter	to wish
décider (de)	to decide (to)
excuser	to excuse

Irregular verbs:

boire (to drink) **dire** (to say, to tell)

Present tense   *Present tense*

je bois	**je dis**
tu bois	**tu dis**
il/elle boit	**il/elle dit**
nous buvons	**nous disons**
vous buvez	**vous dites**
ils/elles boivent	**ils/elles disent**

Perfect tense   *Perfect tense*

j'ai bu, etc.   **j'ai dit**, etc.

CONVERSATION

Hélène prend des résolutions pour la nouvelle année.

Michel   Bonjour, Hélène. Je suis venu vous souhaiter une bonne année.

Hélène   Bonjour, Michel. Bonne année à vous aussi.

Michel   Quoi de neuf?

Hélène   Eh bien, j'ai décidé de changer ma vie. J'ai pris beaucoup de résolutions pour la nouvelle année.

Michel   Vraiment? Et quelles sont ces résolutions?

Hélène   Voici ma liste:
1 Je vais maigrir.
2 Je vais regarder la télévision moins souvent.
3 Je mangerai plus de légumes.
4 Je mangerai plus de fruits.
5 Je dépenserai moins d'argent en vêtements.
Mon mari m'a fait aussi quelques promesses. Voici sa liste:
1 Il va boire moins de bière.
2 Il va boire plus d'eau.
3 Il arrêtera de fumer.
4 Il fera de la gymnastique chaque matin.
5 Il rentrera plus tôt à la maison le soir.

Michel   Et vous pensez que vous serez plus heureux?

Hélène   Oui. Nous aurons plus de temps et plus d'argent. Nous serons tous les deux en meilleure santé.

Michel   Et comment est-ce que vous dépenserez tout et argent?

Hélène   Nous achèterons une voiture neuve. Nous voyagerons à l'étranger plus souvent. Nous irons au Japon. Nous irons en Chine et aux États-Unis. Nous ferons le tour du monde.

Michel   Excusez-moi, mais je dois dire que j'ai déjà entendu ça. Je l'ai entendu l'année dernière. Je ne veux pas vous décourager, mais je suis certain que vous ne ferez jamais rien !

TRANSLATION

Hélène makes (takes) some New Year's resolutions.

Michel	Good morning, Hélène. I've come to wish you a Happy New Year.
Hélène	Good morning, Michel. Happy New Year to you too.
Michel	What's new?
Hélène	Well, I've decided to change my life. I've made a lot of resolutions for the new year.
Michel	Really? And what are these resolutions?
Hélène	Here's my list: 1 I'm going to lose weight. 2 I'm going to watch television less often. 3 I'll eat more vegetables. 4 I'll eat more fruit. 5 I'll spend less money on (*lit.* "in") clothes. My husband has also made a few promises to me. Here's his list: 1 He's going to drink less beer. 2 He's going to drink more water. 3 He'll stop smoking. 4 He'll do exercises each morning. 5 He'll come home earlier in the evening.
Michel	Do you think that you will be happier?
Hélène	Yes. We'll have more time and more money. We'll both (*lit.* "all the two") be in better health.
Michel	And how will you spend all this money?
Hélène	We'll buy a brand-new car. We'll travel abroad more often. We'll go to Japan. We'll go to China and to the United States. We'll tour the world (*lit.* "We'll do the tour of the world").
Michel	I'm sorry (*lit.* "Excuse me"), but I must say that I've already heard that. I heard it last year. I don't want to discourage you, but I'm certain that you will never do anything! (*lit.* "that you will never do nothing.")

Chapter 8

In this chapter, the following elements of grammar are explained:

- the imperfect (past) tense
- relative pronouns ("who/whom/which/that")
- the conditional tense (what we would do, if ...)
- disjunctive pronouns
- the distinction between "**savoir**" and "**connaître**," both meaning "to know"

51 The imperfect tense

We have already seen that the perfect tense is used to talk about the past:

J'ai acheté un livre.

This sentence can be translated "I have bought a book," "I did buy a book," or "I bought a book."

BUT sometimes you will want to say what you used to do at some specific time in your life. On these occasions you have to use the imperfect tense. To form this tense, take the **nous** form of the present tense, drop the **-ons** ending, and add:

je	- ais	**nous**	- ions
tu	- ais	**vous**	- iez
il/elle	- ait	**ils/elles**	- aient

There is only one exception to the previous rule, namely the verb **être**.

Examples:

je fumais	I used to smoke
tu chantais	you *(fam.)* used to sing
il organisait	he used to organize
elle choisissait	she used to choose
nous finissions	we used to finish
vous vendiez	you used to sell
ils lisaient	they used to read
elles écrivaient	they used to write

j'étais	I was
il était	he was
etc.	

j'avais	I had
il avait	he had
etc.	

We also use the imperfect tense when translating such sentences as "I *was reading* the newspaper when the telephone rang." In other words, if the English construction is "was/were ...ing," we require the imperfect tense in French.

Examples:

J'écoutais la radio, quand Michel a téléphoné.
    I was listening to the radio when Michel called.
Elle prenait une douche, quand le facteur est arrivé.
    She was taking a shower when the mailman arrived.

122

Vocabulary

le timbre	stamp
le bruit	noise
le porte-monnaie	purse
le cambrioleur	burglar
la traduction	translation
en haut	upstairs
en bas	downstairs
collectionner	to collect
jouer au football	to play soccer
aller à la pêche	to go fishing
faire de la photo(graphie)	to go in for photography
entrer dans la maison	to enter the house

Exercise 44

Here are some things that Bernard and Marie-Claude used to do when they were younger. Translate using the imperfect tense:

1 He used to play soccer.
2 He used to go fishing.
3 He used to collect stamps.
4 She used to sing.
5 She used to listen to records.

Now translate:

6 We used to learn Spanish.
7 We used to live in a small house.
8 We used to go in for photography.
9 I was finishing the translation when I heard a noise upstairs.
10 She was doing the shopping when she lost her purse.
11 They were watching television when the burglar entered the house.

52 Relative pronouns

Study the following:

qui   who, which, that (subject)
que   whom, which, that (object)
Note: **que** becomes **qu'** in front of a vowel or h.

Examples:

L'automobiliste qui parle français.
    The motorist who speaks French.
La voiture qui est en panne *(f.)*.
    The car that has broken down
    (lit. "which is in breakdown").
L'auto-stoppeur que j'ai pris.
    The hitchhiker whom I picked up.
Le camion que vous avez réparé.
    The truck that you repaired.

If you're having difficulty in deciding whether "who," "which," "that," is the subject or the object, here's a rule to help you:

if, in English, the verb comes immediately after "who," "which," "that," use **qui**

if, in English, there is another word between "who," "which," "that," and the verb, use **que**

Examples:

the car that has broken down   **qui**
the car that I prefer   **que**

Note: in English, the relative pronoun is sometimes omitted, but it must always be expressed in French:

Le moteur que vous vérifiez.
    The engine you are checking.

You will remember that we learned in Chapter 5 that the past participle (**invité, copié, trouvé**) has to reflect the gender and number of the direct object pronouns are used with it. The same principle applies to the relative pronoun **que**:

Voici le permis de conduire que j'ai trouvé.
Here is the driver's license that I found.
Voici la carte que j'ai achetée.
Here's the map that I bought.
Voici les pneus que j'ai choisis.
Here are the tires that I've chosen.

After a preposition "whom" is also translated by **qui**:

Où est le mécanicien à qui vous avez téléphoné?
Where's the mechanic whom you called?
(Where's the mechanic you called?)

BUT "which," after prepositions, is translated as follows:

lequel *(m.)*	**lesquels** *(m. pl.)*
laquelle *(f.)*	**lesquelles** *(f. pl.)*

The above words combine with **à** and **de** in the usual way: **auquel, duquel, desquels, desquelles**. For example:

Le cric avec lequel il a changé la roue.
The jack with which he changed the tire.
La galerie sur laquelle nous avons mis les valises.
The roof rack on which we put the suitcases.
Le garage auquel elle a envoyé son chèque.
The auto-body shop to which she sent her check.

In place of **de qui, duquel, de laquelle, desquels, desquelles**, the French often prefer to use the word **dont**:

L'autoroute dont nous parlons.
The highway that we are speaking of (about).

We also use **dont** to mean "whose":

L'automobiliste dont la femme est malade.
The motorist whose wife is sick.
Le garagiste dont je connais le frère.
The auto-body shop owner whose brother I know.

Note the unexpected word order in the last French sentence. Sometimes "which" in English refers not to a noun, as in our previous examples, but to a whole idea. In these cases use **ce qui** (subject) or **ce que** (object). For example:

Je ne peux pas lire ce qui est écrit ici.
I cannot read what is written here.
Je ne peux pas lire ce que Michel a écrit ici.
I cannot read what Michel has written here.

Vocabulary

le petit déjeuner	breakfast
le poste de télévision	television set
le vestibule	hall
le/la réceptionniste	receptionist
le fils	son
l'ascenseur *(m.)*	elevator
la femme de chambre	chambermaid
la fille	daughter, girl
lourd	heavy
bilingue	bilingual
malade	sick
correct	correct
apporter	to bring
commander	to order
marcher	to walk, to work (machines)
donner sur	to overlook

Exercise 45

Translate:

1 The hotel, that you are looking for, is on the right.
2 I would like the room that overlooks the park.
3 The room, which we have reserved for you, is next to the elevator.
4 I've brought the breakfast that your husband ordered.
5 Where's the television set that doesn't work?

6 The suitcases, which are in the hall, are very heavy.
7 The receptionist (f.), to whom you spoke, is bilingual.
8 The client, whose son is ill, is in room 5.
9 Didn't you understand what the chambermaid said to you?
10 The bill, that you have prepared, is correct.

53 The conditional tense

We use the conditional to say what we *would do, (if)* ... This tense is formed by adding the following endings to the infinitive of the verb:

je	-ais	nous	-ions
tu	-ais	vous	-iez
il/elle	-ait	ils/elles	-aient

As with the future tense, if the infinitive ends in **-re**, omit the final e before adding the endings.

Examples:

je louerais	I would hire
tu inviterais	you *(fam.)* would invite
il habiterait	he would live
elle étudierait	she would study
nous choisirions	we would choose
vous finiriez	you would finish
ils comprendraient	they would understand
elles écriraient	they would write

When a verb is irregular in the future tense, it will have the same irregularity in the conditional tense:

j'aurais	I would have
tu serais	you *(fam.)* would be
il irait	he would go
elle ferait	she would do

nous enverrions	we would send
vous pourriez	you could, would be able
ils voudraient	they would like
elles sauraient	they would know
il faudrait	it would be necessary
il y aurait	there would be

The "if" part of the sentence (i.e. "if I had the time," "if I spoke French," etc.) is expressed in French by **si** (if), followed by the imperfect tense:

si j'avais le temps
  if I had the time
s'il parlait français
  if he spoke French
si vous vendiez votre maison
  if you sold your house

Note: si becomes s' before **il** and **ils**.

The conditional is also used in French when the speaker or writer is repeating something he or she has heard but is unable to vouch for its accuracy. Compare:

Le père a donné son consentement au mariage.
  The father has given his consent to the marriage.
Le père aurait donné son consentement au mariage.
  Apparently, the father has given his consent to the marriage.

Vocabulary

le travail	work
l'interprète *(m. & f.)*	interpreter
l'enfant *(m. & f.)*	child
portugais	Portuguese
marié	married
comme	as
dessiner	to draw

> *Irregular verb:*
>
> **peindre** (to paint)
>
> *Present tense*
>
> **je peins**
> **tu peins**
> **il/elle peint**
> **nous peignons**
> **vous peignez**
> **ils/elles peignent**
>
> *Perfect tense*
>
> **j'ai peint**, etc.

Exercise 46

Answer the questions as follows:

Qu'est-ce que vous feriez, si vous aviez beaucoup de temps?
   What would you do, if you had a lot of time?
   (write a book)
Si j'avais beaucoup de temps, j'écrirais un livre.
   If I had a lot of time, I would write a book.

1   Qu'est-ce que vous feriez, si vous étiez riche?
     (tour the world)
2   Qu'est-ce que vous feriez, si vous ne travailliez pas?
     (paint and draw)
3   Qu'est-ce que Pierre ferait, s'il avait beaucoup de temps?
     (learn Portuguese)
4   Qu'est-ce que Nicole ferait, si elle parlait français?
     (work as an interpreter)
5   Qu'est-ce que Monique ferait, si elle parlait allemand?
     (work as a bilingual secretary)
6   Qu'est-ce que je ferais, si j'étais marié?
     (return home earlier in the evening)

7 Qu'est-ce qu'ils feraient, s'ils étaient en chômage?
(look for work)
8 Qu'est-ce qu'elles feraient, si elles avaient des enfants?
(stay at home)
9 Qu'est-ce que tu ferais, si tu avais le temps?
(read a great deal)
10 Qu'est-ce que nous ferions, si nous voulions maigrir?
(eat less and do exercises)

54 Disjunctive pronouns

We have already seen in Chapter 5 how the French express "me," "him," "her," "to us," "to you," etc., when these pronouns are the object of a verb. But some of these pronouns have a different form when they:

1 follow a preposition
2 form part of a comparison
3 stand alone
4 follow the verb **être** (to be)

Thus:

moi	I, me	**nous**	we, us
toi	you *(fam.)*	**vous**	you
lui	he, him	**eux**	they, them *(m.)*
elle	she, her	**elles**	they, them *(f.)*

Examples:

Est-ce qu'il y a des lettres pour moi?
Are there any letters for me?
Je travaille en face de lui.
I work across from him.
Nous sommes partis sans eux.
We left without them.
Il est plus petit que moi.
He's smaller than I.

Qui parle anglais ici? Elle.
Who speaks English here? She does.
C'est lui qui écrit toutes les lettres.
It's he who writes all the letters.

Vocabulary

le président	president
le programmeur	computer programmer
le poste de radio	radio (set)
le traité	treaty
la dactylo	typist
la femme de ménage	daily help
travailleur, travailleuse (f.)	hardworking
paresseux, paresseuse (f.)	lazy
casser	to break

Exercise 47

Replace the words in italics with a pronoun:

1 Je suis arrivé avec *Paul*.
2 Je voudrais avoir une place à côté de *la secrétaire*.
3 Nous avons l'intention de partir sans *Pierre et Monique*.
4 Anne est plus travailleuse que *les nouvelles dactylos*.
5 Michel est moins paresseux que *le nouveau programmeur*.
6 Qui a cassé mon poste de radio? *La femme de ménage*.
7 C'est *le président et le premier ministre* qui ont signé le
   traité hier.

55 The verbs "savoir" and "connaître"

In Chapter 7 we learned that "to know" is translated **savoir**.
This verb means to know a fact:

Savez-vous où est Paul?
    Do you know where Paul is?
Je sais à quelle heure le train part.
    I know at what time the train leaves.

BUT, when we talk about knowing a person or a place, that is
to say, when the meaning is "to be acquainted with," then we
must use the irregular verb **connaître**:

Present tense

je connais I know, I am acquainted with
tu connais
il/elle connaît
nous connaissons
vous connaissez
ils/elles connaissent

Past tense (perfect): **j'ai connu**, I knew, I was acquainted with

Examples:

Je connais Paul, mais je ne sais pas où il habite.
    I know Paul, but I don't know where he lives.
Vous connaissez Paris?
    Do you know Paris?

Vocabulary

l'oncle	uncle
la tante	aunt
la machine à écrire	typewriter
libre	free
occupé	busy

132

Exercise 48

Translate:

1 I don't know if Paul has finished his work.
2 I don't know the Duponts.
3 Do you know where I can rent a typewriter?
4 Do you know if the doctor is free?
5 Does Marie-Claude know my aunt?

Exercise 49

*In the conversation at the end of this chapter, change all the familiar forms (**tu, te, toi, ton**) into the more formal **vous/votre** forms and make all necessary changes to the verbs.*

Vocabulary

le cas	case, situation
les gens (*m. pl.*)	people
la visite	visit
la porte	door
la retraite	retirement
au-dessus de	above
chez	at someone's home or store
bonsoir	good evening
justement	just
si	so; yes (emphatic use after a negative)
à propos	by the way
à mi-temps	part time
tout de suite	immediately
trop	too
inattendu	unexpected
bruyant	noisy
déranger	to disturb
arranger	to suit
frapper	to knock
penser à	to think of (thoughts)
penser de	to think of (opinion)
espérer	to hope (see section 81, Chapter 12 for how **espérer** slightly changes its spelling in the present tense)

CONVERSATION

Une visite inattendue

Pierre   Bonsoir Nicole, j'espère que je ne te dérange pas.

Nicole   Pierre! Bonsoir. Je pensais justement à toi.

Pierre   Tu n'es pas trop occupée?

Nicole   Non, non. J'écrivais une lettre, quand tu as frappé à la porte.

Pierre   Ah bon? A qui est-ce que tu écrivais?

Nicole   Aux Dupont.

Pierre   Les Dupont? Je ne les connais pas.

Nicole   Mais si! Les Dupont sont les gens qui habitaient au-dessus de chez nous à Paris, qui voyageaient beaucoup et dont les enfants étaient si bruyants.

Pierre   Ah oui. Je ne les connaissais pas très bien. À propos, comment va ton travail?

Nicole   Pas trop bien. Si seulement je pouvais travailler à mi-temps, ça m'arrangerait bien.

Pierre   Qu'est-ce que tu ferais de tout ce temps libre?

Nicole   Je peindrais, je dessinerais. Michel et moi, nous sortirions plus souvent, nous irions au cinéma, au restaurant. Je ferais du sport, j'apprendrais l'anglais, je lirais tous les livres que j'ai achetés l'année dernière, je …

Pierre   Tu ferais mieux de prendre ta retraite tout de suite!

TRANSLATION

An unexpected visit

Pierre   Good evening, Nicole, I hope that I'm not disturbing you.

Nicole   Pierre! Good evening. I was just thinking of you.

Pierre   You're not too busy?

Nicole   No, no. I was writing a letter when you knocked at the door.

Pierre   Really? (*lit.* "oh, good?") Who were you writing to?

Nicole   To the Duponts (*lit.* "To the Dupont").

Pierre   The Duponts? I don't know them.

Nicole   Yes, you do! The Duponts are the people who used to live above us (*lit.* "above at our place") in Paris, who used to travel a great deal, and whose children were so noisy.

Pierre   Oh yes. I didn't know them very well (*lit.* "I used not to know them very well"). By the way, how's your work going?

Nicole   Not too well. If only I could work part time, that would suit me well.

Pierre   What would you do with (*lit.* "of") all this free time?

Nicole   I would paint, I would draw. Michel and I (*lit.* "Michel and I, we") would go out more often, we would go to the movies, to a restaurant. I'd play sports (*lit.* "I'd do some sports"), I'd learn English, I'd read all the books I bought last year, I …

Pierre   You would do better to retire immediately! (*lit.* "You would do better to take your retirement immediately.")

Self-Assessment Test 2

This Self-Assessment Test, based on Lessons 5-8, allows you to check on your progress and to see whether any revision is needed. Deduct one point for every grammatical mistake or misspelling. The answers and score assessment are in the Key.

A: Prepositions   Total: 8 points

Complete the following:

1 Il y a un taxi [in front of] l'hôtel.
2 Il y a un restaurant [next to] la banque.
3 Il y a une librairie [opposite] l'université.
4 Il y a un tunnel [under] la Manche.
5 Est-ce qu'il y a une cabine téléphonique [near] la gare?
6 C'est difficile de travailler [without] ma secrétaire.
7 Nous pouvons manger [after] le spectacle.
8 Téléphonez [before] neuf heures.

B: The perfect tense   Total: 10 points

Imagine the following: You are a journalist (male or female).This morning you arrived at the hotel at seven o'clock. You went to an international conference at ten o'clock. You left very late. Now complete these sentences:

1 Je suis j____.
2 Ce m____, je ____ ____ à l'hôtel à sept heures.
3 Je ____ ____ a une c____ i____ à dix heures.
4 Je ____ ____ très t____.

C: The weather   Total: 10 points

Suggest the likely weather at the times and in the places indicated:

1   En Grande-Bretagne, au mois d'avril.
2   À Nice, au mois d'août.
3   À Londres, au mois de novembre.
4   En Russie, au mois de décembre.
5   En Écosse, en hiver.

D: Countries   Total: 12 points

Below are some simple clues to the names of countries. Identify the country and give its French name.

1   Son porto est très bon.
2   Le mont Fuji-Yama.
3   La statue de la Liberté.
4   La capitale? Athènes.
5   Cervantès.
6   Léonard de Vinci.
7   Ses tulipes sont belles.
8   La Révolution culturelle.
9   La capitale? Bruxelles.
10 Liberté, Egalité, Fraternité.
11 Shakespeare.
12 La capitale? Copenhague.

E: Numerals   Total: 14 points

Complete the following, writing the totals in words:

a)   30 + 28
b)   40 + 30
c)   15 + 60
d)   40 + 43
e)   50 + 40
f)   10 + 89
g)   50 + 50

F: The imperfect tense   Total: 14 points

Talk about your French friends, Hélène and Pierre:

1 He used to play soccer.
2 She used to learn English.
3 They used to live in a large house.
4 They were shopping when she lost her purse.

G: The conditional tense   Total: 8 points

"If only ... ". Answer the questions as indicated:

1 Qu'est-ce que vous feriez, si vous étiez riche?
   [visit Japan and China]
2 Qu'est-ce que Monique ferait, si elle parlait italien?
   [work as a bilingual secretary]
3 Qu'est-ce que je ferais, si j'étais au chômage?
   [look for work – use "tu"]
4 Qu'est-ce que nous ferions, si nous avions beaucoup de
   temps?
     [read a lot – use "nous"s]

H: Do you remember...?   Total: 4 points

*(a) What's the difference between the verbs **savoir** and
connaître, both meaning "to know?"*
*(b) What's the difference in meaning between **je ne sais pas
jouer du piano** and **je ne peux pas jouer du piano**?*

I: Conversation (Role-play)   Total: 20 points

Play the part of Hélène in this dialogue:

> *Hélène:* I've decided to change my life. I'm going to
>   watch television less often. I'll eat more fruit.
>   I'll do exercises each morning. I'll spend less
>   money on clothes.
> *Michel:* Tu penses que tu seras plus heureuse?
> *Hélène:* Yes, I'll have more time and more money,
>   and I'll be in better health.

Chapter 9

Here, the main topics are demonstrative pronouns ("this one," "that one," "these," "those") and possessive pronouns ("mine," "yours," "hers," etc.). Also study:

- more interrogative words and formations
- more about adverbs and adverbial expressions
- another quartet of irregular verbs

56 Demonstrative pronouns

In English, a sentence like "I prefer my doctor to the doctor who came this morning" would normally be shortened to "I prefer my doctor to the one who came this morning." In French, we express "the one," "those" as follows:

celui *(m.)*	the one
ceux *(m. pl.)*	those
celle *(f.)*	the one
celles *(f. pl.)*	those

Examples:

Je préfère mon médecin à celui qui est venu ce matin.
  I prefer my doctor to the one who came this morning.
Cette infirmière et celle qui a pris votre tension.
  This nurse and the one who took your blood pressure.
J'ai apporté vos comprimés et ceux de votre mari.
  I've brought your tablets and your husband's (lit. "those of your husband").

We would normally change "this dentist and that dentist" to "this dentist and that one." In French, "this one," "that one," "these," "those" become:

masculine		*feminine*	
celui-ci	this one	**celle-ci**	this one
celui-là	that one	**celle-là**	that one
ceux-ci	these	**celles-ci**	these
ceux-là	those	**celles-là**	those

Examples:

Cet hôpital-ci ou celui-là?
    This hospital or that one?
Quelle ambulance préférez-vous, celle-ci ou celle-là?
    Which ambulance do you prefer, this one or that one?
Quels médicaments prenez-vous, ceux-ci ou ceux-là?
    Which medicines do you take, these or those?

If you prefer not to refer to an object by name but to call it simply "this" or "that," you can use the following words:

ceci	this
cela (or **ça**)	that

Examples:

Je voudrais acheter ceci. I'd like to buy this.
Le (or la) malade m'a donné cela. The patient gave me that.

"This," "that," "these," "those," followed by the verb "to be," are all normally translated by **c'est** or **ce sont**:

C'est votre petit déjeuner, Monsieur.
    This is your breakfast, sir.
Ce sont (or c'est) les ordonnances que vous avez demandées.
    These are the prescriptions you asked for.

C'est, ce sont can also mean "he/she is" and "they are":

C'est un dentiste (or Il est dentiste). He's a dentist.

Vocabulary

le rhume	cold
le coeur	heart
le prince	prince
le chirurgien	surgeon
le/la kinésithérapeute	physical therapist
le pharmacien	pharmacist
le rendez-vous	appointment
la greffe	transplant
la soeur	sister
la princesse	princess
la pharmacienne	pharmacist
moderne	modern
effectuer	to carry out

Exercise 50

Translate:

1 My cold is worse than my sister's.
2 This hospital is more modern than the one the princess visited last year.
3 Which surgeon carried out the heart transplant? This one or that one?
4 Do you have an appointment with this dentist or that one?
5 The physical therapist gave me this.
6 The pharmacist prepared that.
7 This is your new secretary.
8 These are your patients.

57 Possessive pronouns

Instead of saying "The waiter has brought your soup but not my soup," we would usually say, "The waiter has brought your soup but not *mine*." In French, possessive pronouns ("mine," "yours," "hers," etc.) must agree with the noun they replace and are expressed as follows:

Pronouns replacing masculine nouns

singular	*plural*	
le mien	les miens	mine
le tien	les tiens	yours *(fam.)*
le sien	les siens	his/hers
le nôtre	les nôtres	ours
le vôtre	les vôtres	yours
le leur	les leurs	theirs

Pronouns replacing feminine nouns

singular	*plural*	
la mienne	les miennes	mine
la tienne	les tiennes	yours *(fam.)*
la sienne	les siennes	his/hers
la nôtre	les nôtres	ours
la vôtre	les vôtres	yours
la leur	les leurs	theirs

Examples:

Le garçon a apporté votre soupe, mais pas la mienne.
    The waiter has brought your soup, but not mine.
Voici son croissant, mais où est le vôtre?
    Here's his/her croissant, but where's yours?
Notre jambon est très bon; comment est le leur?
    Our ham is very good; how's theirs?
Ma bière est excellente; est-ce que la vôtre est bonne aussi?
    My beer is excellent; is yours good too?
J'ai payé mon café, mais je n'ai pas payé les leurs.
    I've paid for my coffee, but I haven't paid for theirs.

When following the verb "to be" and having the meaning of "belonging to," the possessive pronouns are often translated by:

à moi	à nous
à toi	à vous
à lui	à eux *(m. pl.)*
à elle	à elles *(f. pl.)*

It is also possible to say **à Pierre, à ma femme,** etc., meaning Pierre's, my wife's:

Pardon, Madame, est-ce que ce parapluie est à vous?
Excuse me, madam, is this umbrella yours?
Ces gants *(m.)* **ne sont pas à moi; ils sont à mon frère.**
These gloves are not mine; they belong to my brother.

58 More interrogatives

WHAT ... ? is expressed as follows:

a) After a preposition, use **quoi:**

À quoi pensez-vous?
What are you thinking about?
Je pense à mon déjeuner.
I'm thinking about my lunch.
Avec quoi avez-vous payé le dîner?
What did you pay for the dinner with?
J'ai payé avec ma carte de crédit.
I paid with my credit card.

b) After the verb "to be" and a noun, use **quel, quelle, quels, quelles:**

Quel est votre nom?
What is your name?
Quel est votre numéro de téléphone?
What is your telephone number?

Quelle est votre adresse?
  What is your address?
Quels sont les prix?
  What are the prices?

c) When subject of the sentence, use **qu'est-ce qui**:

Délicieux? Qu'est-ce qui est délicieux?
  Delicious? What's delicious?

d) When object of the sentence, use **qu'est-ce que**
or **que (qu')**:

Qu'est-ce que vous avez comme légumes?
or **Qu'avez-vous comme légumes?**
  What have you got in the way of vegetables?

e) As an exclamation, "What!" is translated **Quoi!**:

Quoi! Le service n'est pas compris?
  What! The tip isn't included ?
Quoi! Le bar est fermé? What! The bar is closed?
Quoi! Le café n'est pas ouvert? What! The café isn't open?

f) As an exclamation, "what" followed by a noun is translated
by **quel, quelle, quels, quelles**:

Quel repas! Quelle cuisinière!
  What a meal! What a cook!

WHO, WHOM … ? is expressed as follows (see also Ch. 3):

a) When subject of the sentence, use **qui** or **qui est-ce qui**:

Qui est-ce qui a réservé la table? Who reserved the table?

b) When object of the sentence, use **qui** or **qui est-ce que**:

Qui est-ce que vous avez payé? La serveuse?
  Whom did you pay? The waitress?
Avec qui avez-vous mangé?
  Who(m) did you eat with?

WHICH ONE(S) ... ? is expressed by **lequel, laquelle, lesquels, lesquelles:**

Voici trois bons vins. À votre avis, lequel est le meilleur?
Here are three good wines. In your opinion, which one is the best?
Toutes les tables sont libres, Madame; laquelle préférez-vous?
All the tables are free, madam; which one do you prefer?
Des légumes? Oui, lesquels voulez-vous?
Vegetables? Yes, which would you like?

We saw in Chapter 3 that "Which book?", "Which house?", etc., are translated **Quel livre?, Quelle maison?,** etc. For example:

À quel restaurant avez-vous l'intention d'aller?
Which restaurant do you intend to go to?

But remember that in French the past participle of a verb conjugated with **avoir** takes the same gender and number as the direct object, when this direct object precedes the past participle (see also Chapter 5):

Quel vin avez-vous bu?
Which wine did you drink?
Quelle viande avez-vous mangée?
Which meat did you eat?
Quels plats avez-vous recommandés?
Which dishes did you recommend?
Quelles pommes avez-vous achetées?
Which apples did you buy?

WHOSE ...? is translated by **à qui:**

À qui est ce dessert?
Whose is this dessert?
À qui est cette serviette?
Whose is this napkin?

Vocabulary

le barman	bartender
le whisky	whiskey
le poisson	fish
le repas	meal
le couteau	knife
le chapeau	hat
la fourchette	fork
la cuillère	spoon
les baguettes *(f.)*	chopsticks
frais, fraîche *(f.)*	fresh
chinois	Chinese
italien	Italian
commander	to order

Irregular verbs:

sentir (to smell)   **servir** (to serve)

Present tense   *Present tense*

je sens	**je sers**
tu sens	**tu sers**
il/elle sent	**il/elle sert**
nous sentons	**nous servons**
vous sentez	**vous servez**
ils/elles sentent	**ils/elles serven**

partir (to leave)

Present tense

je pars
tu pars
il/elle part
nous partons
vous partez
ils/elles partent

Note: **payer** (to pay) is not irregular, but is one of those verbs that changes its spelling in the stem (see section 81). As seen in the following present tense, **y** becomes **i** before a silent **e**.

je paie	nous payons
tu paies	vous payez
il/elle paie	ils/elles paient

Exercise 51

Translate:

1 The bartender has served you your whiskey, but where's mine?
2 My fish is delicious; yours is not fresh.
3 I've paid our check and they've paid theirs.
4 Does this hat belong to you or to your friend *(m.)*?
5 What do you want to eat this Chinese meal with? With chopsticks? What! No! With a knife and fork.
6 What is the telephone number of the Italian restaurant?
7 Which vegetables did she order?
8 What smells so good?
9 Here's a list of the best restaurants in Paris; which one do you prefer?
10 Whose spoon is this?

---

59 More adverbs

We can form adverbs from adjectives ending in **-ant, -ent**, by changing the **-nt** to **-mment**:

constant becomes **constamment** "constantly"
évident becomes **évidemment** "obviously"

Note: an important exception is **lent, lentement** "slowly."

A few adjectives can be used as adverbs without any change:

La soupe sent bon. The soup smells good.
Le poisson sent mauvais. The fish smells bad.
Frappez fort. Knock loudly.
Parlez plus bas. Speak more softly.

Here is a list of useful adverbs and adverbial expressions (see also Chapter 5):

Time

tôt	early
tard	late
maintenant	now
tout de suite	immediately
immédiatement	immediately
ensuite	afterwards
toujours	always, still
hier	yesterday
aujourd'hui	today
demain	tomorrow
ce matin	this morning
cet après-midi	this afternoon
ce soir	this evening
souvent	often
rarement	rarely

Place

ici	here
là	here, there
là-bas	over there
à droite	on/to the right
à gauche	on/to the left
en haut	upstairs
en bas	downstairs
partout	everywhere

Certainty

sûrement	certainly, surely
certainement	certainly

Doubt

peut-être	perhaps
probablement	probably

Manner

bien	well
mal	badly
ensemble	together
surtout	especially
exprès	on purpose
vite	quickly
rapidement	rapidly
lentement	slowly
déjà	already
encore	still, yet

60 Position of adverbs

In French, adverbs are placed after the verb, never between the subject and verb, as in English:

Il parle rarement anglais. He rarely speaks English.
Elle va souvent au théâtre. She often goes to the theater.

In compound tenses (e.g. the perfect tense) the following adverbs are normally placed between **avoir** (or **être**) and the past participle:

bien	**toujours**
mal	**souvent**
vite	**beaucoup**
encore	**déjà**

Examples:

Vous avez bien répondu à la question.
   You have answered the question well.
Je n'ai pas encore lu votre lettre.
   I haven't read your letter yet.
Votre frère est déjà parti?
   Has your brother already left?

But when the adverb is an important word in the sentence, it generally comes at the end:

Je vais écrire la lettre maintenant.
   I'm going to write the letter now.

Vocabulary

le bain	bath
neiger	to snow
pleuvoir	to rain
taper à la machine	to type

Exercise 52

Give the opposite of:

1 Elle tape vite à la machine.
2 Ils chantent bien.
3 Ne parlez pas si fort.
4 Il va rarement chez ses parents.
5 Nous n'avons pas encore mangé.
6 Il va peut-être pleuvoir ou neiger.
7 Elle prend un bain en haut.
8 Elles feront les courses demain.

Vocabulary

le mariage	wedding, marriage
le mannequin	model, dummy
la veste	jacket
la taille	size
la couleur	color
la mode	fashion
la laine	wool
la vitrine	store window
la vente	sale
bleu marine	navy blue
gris clair	light gray
pur	pure
court	short
long, longue (f.)	long
(mal)heureusement	(un)fortunately
exactement	exactly
le dernier cri	the latest fashion
être en train de	to be in the middle of (doing something)
essayer	to try, to try on
ne . . (verb) . . que	only

Irregular verb:

plaire (to please)

Present tense

je plais
tu plais
il/elle plaît
nous plaisons
vous plaisez
ils/elles plaisent

Perfect tense

j'ai plu, etc.

CONVERSATION

Une veste dernier cri

Client Bonjour, Madame. Je vais à un mariage la semaine prochaine ... heureusement pas le mien ... et je voudrais acheter une veste ... une veste très chic ... une veste dernier cri.

Vendeuse Oui, quelle est votre taille, Monsieur?

Client Aux États-Unis je fais du 42.

Vendeuse Quelle couleur préférez-vous?

Client Je veux surtout une couleur à la mode.

Vendeuse Eh bien, j'ai cette veste-ci en bleu marine en pure laine, et celle-là en gris clair.

Client Hm, j'aurais préféré une veste comme celle que vous avez en vitrine. Elle me plaît beaucoup.

Vendeuse Malheureusement, je n'ai plus votre taille, Monsieur. Je n'ai que des petites tailles.

Client Et celle sur le mannequin, ici dans le magasin?

Vendeuse C'est aussi une petite taille. Je pense qu'elle sera trop courte pour vous.

Client Mais ... regardez! Regardez celle-là! C'est exactement ce qu'il me faut. Je vais l'essayer tout de suite.

Vendeuse Non, non, non, Monsieur! Cette veste-là n'est pas en vente. Elle est à ce monsieur là-bas qui est en train d'essayer un costume!

TRANSLATION

The latest thing in jackets
(lit. "A jacket latest cry")

Customer Good morning. I'm going to a wedding next week ... fortunately not mine ... and I'd like to buy a jacket ... a very stylish jacket ... the latest thing in jackets.

Assistant Yes, what is your size, Sir?

Customer In the United States I take size 42 (*lit.* "I do some 42").

Assistant What color do you prefer?

Customer I particularly want a color that's in fashion.

Assistant Well, I have this jacket in navy blue in pure wool, and that one in light gray.

Customer Hm, I would have preferred a jacket like the one you have in the window. I like it very much (*lit.* "It pleases me much").

Assistant Unfortunately, I no longer have your size, Sir. I only have small sizes.

Customer What about (*lit.* "And") the one which is on the model, here in the shop?

Assistant That's also a small size. I think it will be too short for you.

Customer But ... look! Look at that one! That's exactly what I need. I'm going to try it on right away.

Assistant No, no, no, Sir, that jacket is not for sale! It belongs to that gentleman over there who's trying on a suit!

Chapter 10

You are introduced to reflexive verbs ("**se laver**," "to wash oneself," as distinct from "**laver**," "to wash," etc.). Other topics include:

- verbs preceded by prepositions
- the translation of "to" before an infinitive
- the pronouns "**en**," "**y**," "**on**"

61 Reflexive verbs

Study the following:

laver	to wash	se laver	to wash oneself
raser	to shave	se raser	to shave oneself
brûler	to burn	se brûler	to burn oneself
perdre	to lose	se perdre	to lose oneself
couper	to cut	se couper	to cut oneself
préparer	to prepare	se préparer	to prepare oneself
amuser	to amuse	s'amuser	to enjoy oneself
habiller	to dress	s'habiller	to dress oneself

The verbs in the second column are being used reflexively and are conjugated as follows:

Present tense

je me lave	I wash myself
tu te rases	you (*fam.*) shave yourself
il se brûle	he burns himself
elle se prépare	she prepares herself

nous nous amusons	we enjoy ourselves
vous vous habillez	you dress yourself (yourselves)
ils se perdent	they (m.) lose themselves
elles se coupent	they (f.) cut themselves

Note: **me, te,** and **se** become **m', t',** and **s'** before a vowel or h.

- All reflexive verbs form their compound tenses with **être.** The past participle agrees in gender and number with the preceding direct object.

Perfect tense

je me suis lavé(e)	I washed myself
tu t'es habillé(e)	you (fam.) dressed yourself
il s'est rasé	he shaved himself
elle ne s'est pas amusée	she did not enjoy herself
nous nous sommes préparé(e)s	we prepared ourselves
vous ne vous êtes pas perdu(e)	you didn't lose yourself
vous ne vous êtes pas perdu(e)s	you didn't lose yourselves
ils se sont brûlés	they burned themselves
elles ne se sont pas coupées	they didn't cut themselves

Imperfect tense
je me lavais   I used to wash or I was washing myself

Future tense
je me laverai   I will wash myself

Conditional tense
je me laverais   I would wash myself

Note that in English we don't always add the reflexive pronoun, but say simply "I wash," "he shaves." In French the reflexive pronoun must always be expressed. Compare:

Je me rase. I shave.
Je rase mon père. I shave my father.

- Reflexive verbs are much more common in French than in English. Here is a list for reference:

se déshabiller	to undress oneself
s'endormir	to fall asleep
se réveiller	to wake up
se lever	to get up
se dépêcher	to hurry
se promener	to go for a walk
se reposer	to rest
se coucher	to go to bed
se tromper	to make a mistake
s'appeler	to be called
se marier	to get married
se débarrasser de	to get rid of
se servir de	to make use of
se souvenir de	to remember

- It is important to distinguish between reflexive pronouns and pronouns that are merely used for emphasis. Compare:

Je lave les enfants. I wash the children.
Je me lave. I wash myself.
Je lave les enfants moi-même. I wash the children myself.

These emphatic pronouns are:

moi-même	nous-mêmes
toi-même	vous-même(s)
lui-même	eux-mêmes
elle-même	elles-mêmes

Vocabulary

se peigner	to comb one's hair
se maquiller	to put on one's makeup
se laver les mains (f.)	to wash one's hands
se brosser les dents (f.)	to brush one's teeth

Exercise 53

This is what Paul does each day.

Translate:

1 He wakes up at 7 A.M.
2 He washes.
3 He shaves.
4 He goes to work.

And now Monique:

5 She gets up at 8 A.M.
6 She takes a shower.
7 She combs her hair.
8 She puts her makeup on.
9 She goes to the station.

This is what you and I do:

10 We wash.
11 We dress quickly.
12 We go for a walk.
13 We go to bed at 10 P.M.

Translate:

14 I *(f.)* have enjoyed myself.
15 You *(f.)* have not made a mistake.
16 They *(f.)* are resting.
17 They *(m.)* have washed the car themselves.
18 We brush our teeth each morning.

---

* Reflexive pronouns are also used in sentences where we use the expression "each other":

Nous nous sommes souvent rencontrés.
   We often met.
Les Américains et les Chinois ne se comprennent pas.
   The Americans and the Chinese do not understand each other.

- Note that the past participle of reflexive verbs does not agree with a preceding *indirect* object (i.e. when the meaning is *to* or *for* myself, himself, etc.). Compare:

  Ils se sont rencontrés. They met each other.
  Ils se sont téléphoné. They called (to) each other.

62 Verbs preceded by prepositions

Study the following:

a) I'm used to *getting up* very early.
b) He left *without saying* good-bye.
c) She hesitated *before replying*.
d) *After buying* a computer, he worked much more quickly.
e) These cassettes are excellent *for improving* one's pronunciation.
f) He began *by criticizing* the managing director.

You will have noticed that, in English, verbs preceded by a preposition end in -ing. In French, the infinitive is used:

a) **Je suis habitué à me lever très tôt.**
b) **Il est parti sans dire au revoir.**
c) **Elle a hésité avant de répondre.**
d) **Après avoir acheté un ordinateur, il a travaillé beaucoup plus vite.**
e) **Ces cassettes sont excellentes pour améliorer sa prononciation.**
f) **Il a commencé par critiquer le président-directeur général.**

There is one exception to the above rule; namely, the preposition **en**, which is followed by the present participle. This will be dealt with in the next chapter.

Note also that, although the English is usually "after buying," etc., the French has to be "after having bought," **après avoir acheté** or, in the case of those verbs conjugated with **être, après être ...**

Vocabulary

le mot	word
le ménage	housework
l'électricien *(m.)*	electrician
la lampe	lamp
l'émission *(f.)*	broadcast
partir	to leave
quitter	to leave (with object)
capter	to pick up (broadcast)
tout le monde	everyone

Exercise 54

Translate:

1 He left the house without saying a word.
2 She's used to listening to records in her bedroom.
3 Before repairing the lamp, he telephoned the electrician.
4 After preparing breakfast, she did the housework.
5 My mother began by saying that the family was in good health and finished by wishing everyone a happy new year.
6 This radio is excellent for picking up French broadcasts.

63 Translation of "to" before an infinitive

Compare the following French and English sentences:

a) **Je dois apprendre le français.**
  I have to learn French.
b) **J'ai décidé d'apprendre le français.**
  I have decided to learn French.
c) **J'ai commencé à apprendre le français.**
  I have started to learn French.
d) **J'ai acheté ce livre pour apprendre le français.**
  I have bought this book to learn French.

You will see from the above sentences that "to" coming before an infinitive is sometimes:

a) not translated
b) translated by **de (d')**
c) translated by **à**
d) translated by **pour**

Unfortunately, there is only one rule to help us decide which preposition to use and it's this: when "to" means "in order to," use **pour**.

The rest of the time it's simply a question of memorizing which verbs take no preposition, which take **de**, and which take **à**.
Here are some lists for reference (see Hugo's "French Verbs Simplified" for complete lists), followed by a few model sentences.

• "To" is not translated before an infinitive coming after these verbs:

aimer	to like, to love
préférer	to prefer
vouloir	to want
désirer	to wish
aller	to go
venir	to come

devoir	to have to
falloir (il faut)	to be necessary
espérer	to hope
pouvoir	to be able
savoir	to know how

- "To" is translated by **de** before an infinitive coming after these verbs:

cesser	to stop
conseiller	to advise
décider	to decide
demander	to ask
dire	to tell
empêcher	to prevent
essayer	to try to avoid
éviter	to finish
finir	to finish
oublier	to forget
permettre	to allow
persuader	to persuade
promettre	to promise
proposer	to propose
refuser	to refuse
regretter	to regret

Note also:

être content de	to be pleased to
être heureux de	to be happy to
être ravi de	to be delighted to
être triste de	to be sad to
être désolé de	to be sorry to
avoir l'intention de	to intend to
avoir l'occasion de	to have the opportunity to
avoir le temps de	to have the time to
avoir le plaisir de	to have the pleasure to
il est facile de	it is easy to
il est difficile de	it is difficult to
il est possible de	it is possible to
il est impossible de	it is impossible to

il est permis de	it is permitted to
il est défendu de	it is forbidden to
il est temps de	it is time to

* *"To"* is translated by **à** before an infinitive coming after these verbs:

aider	to help
apprendre	to learn
avoir	to have
commencer	to begin
continuer	to continue
encourager	to encourage
enseigner	to teach
hésiter	to hesitate
inviter	to invite
réussir	to succeed

Note also:

être prêt à	to be ready to
être disposé à	to be willing to
avoir de la difficulté à	to have difficulty in
avoir du mal à	to have difficulty in

Examples:

Je préfère aller me baigner.
 I prefer to go for a swim.
Nous espérons aller à la plage cet après-midi.
 We hope to go to the beach this afternoon.
Ils ont décidé de louer un pédalo.
 They have decided to rent a pedal boat.
Je vous conseille de faire une promenade en bateau.
 I advise you to go on a boat trip.
Nous sommes contents de voir le soleil.
 We are pleased to see the sun .
Avez-vous réussi à trouver des chaises longues?
 Did you succeed in finding some lounge chairs?
Nous l'avons aidée à chercher des coquillages *(m.).*
 We helped her to look for some shells.
Il est temps de rentrer à l'hôtel.
 It's time to return to the hotel.

162

Vocabulary

l'excursion (f.)	excursion
les lunettes (f.) de soleil	sunglasses
faire du ski nautique	to go waterskiing
faire de la planche à voile	to go windsurfing

Exercise 55

Complete the following:

1 (I intend to) acheter des lunettes de soleil.
2 (Will it be possible to) faire des excursions?
3 (We prefer to) louer un appartement.
4 (They *(m.)* invited me *(f.)* to) aller à la pêche.
5 (I hesitate to) faire du ski nautique.
6 (Will you have the opportunity to) faire de la planche à voile?

64 Direct object and indirect object pronouns together

Sometimes two object pronouns appear together in the same sentence. Notice that **le, la, l', les** follow **me, vous, nous:**

Paul me le donne. Paul gives it to me.
Nicole nous la vend. Nicole sells it to us.
Je vous les enverrai. I'll send them to you.

But **le, la, l', les** precede **lui** and **leur:**

Nous le lui avons déjà montré.
  We have already shown it to him (or to her).
Vous la leur avez donnée?
  Did you give it to them?

Je ne les lui ai pas vendus.
I didn't sell them to him (or to her).

Vocabulary

le dossier	file
le/la collègue	colleague
le télex	telex
la moto	motorcycle
la facture	invoice

Exercise 56

Replace all nouns with pronouns (and make any necessary changes):

1 Est-ce que vous m'avez donné le dossier?
2 Notre directeur nous a promis les deux voitures.
3 Mon collègue a l'intention de me vendre ses disques.
4 J'ai envoyé un télex à Paul.
5 Pierre montre sa nouvelle moto à Monique.
6 Nous avons donné les factures aux clients.

65 The pronoun "en"

En replaces a word or an idea introduced by **de**. En means:

a) some or any, when not followed by a noun:

Avez-vous des journaux américains?
Do you have any American newspapers?
Oui, nous en avons. Yes, we have some.
Non, nous n'en avons pas. No, we don't have any.

Note that "some," "any" must be expressed in French, even if omitted in English:

Avez-vous des enveloppes *(f.)***?** Do you have any envelopes?
Oui, j'en ai. Yes, I have.

b) of it, of them:

Avez-vous acheté de l'essence *(f.)***?** Did you buy any gas?
Oui, j'en ai acheté beaucoup. Yes, I bought a lot (of it).
Ont-ils des enfants? Do they have any children?
Oui, ils en ont deux. Yes, they have two (of them).

c) about it, about them

Avez-vous parlé de la navette spatiale?
    Did you talk about (of) the space shuttle?
Oui, tous les astronautes en parlent!
    Yes, all the astronauts are talking about it!

d) from there

Est-ce que les ingénieurs vont au centre de contrôle?
    Are the engineers going to the control center?
Non, ils en viennent.
    No, they've just come (lit. "they come") from there.

66 The pronoun "y"

Y replaces a word or an idea introduced by **à**. **Y** means:

a) there:

Est-ce que Paul connaît les États-Unis?
    Does Paul know the United States?
Oui, il y a passé trois ans.
    Yes, he spent three years there.

Est-ce que tu viens de la gare?
    Are you *(fam.)* coming from the station?
Non, j'y vais.
    No, I'm going there.

Note: when actually pointing, we use **là** or **là-bas**.

b) to it, to them:

Il faut toujours faire la queue à Moscou.
    One always has to wait in line in Moscow.
Oui, mais les Russes y sont habitués.
    Yes, but the Russians are used to it.

Note that **y** cannot be omitted:

Est-ce que le directeur est dans son bureau?
    Is the director in his office?
Oui, il y est.
    Yes, he is.

67 The indefinite pronoun "on"

In English, when referring to people in general, we use words like "one," "they," "you," "people;" e.g., "In England one drives on the left" or "In China they eat with chopsticks." In sentences like these, the French use the pronoun **on**, followed by the third person singular of the verb:

En Angleterre on roule à gauche.
    In England they drive on the left.
En Chine on mange avec des baguettes.
    In China they eat with chopsticks.
On dit qu'il parle sept langues.
    People say he speaks seven languages.

On is often used to translate the English passive:

On a invité les diplomates chinois à l'Ambassade de France.
The Chinese diplomats have been invited to the French Embassy.

Informally in conversation, the French often use **on** in place of **nous**:

Alors, on va partir aujourd'hui ou demain?
Well, are we going to leave today or tomorrow?

Note: **on** sometimes becomes **l'on** after **et** and **si**; the French find this sound more pleasant to the ear.

Vocabulary

le banc	bench
l'attitude	attitude
la promotion	promotion
la chance	luck
portatif, portative (f.)	portable
sociable	sociable
récemment	recently
encore	again
bien sûr	of course
alors	well
lorsque	when
perfectionner	to perfect
apprécier	to appreciate
s'acheter	to buy for oneself

Irregular verbs:

s'asseoir (to sit down)

Present tense
je m'assieds
tu t'assieds
il/elle s'assied
nous nous asseyons
vous vous asseyez
ils/elles s'asseyent

Perfect tense
je me suis assis, etc.

Future tense
je m'assiérai, etc.

sortir (to go out)

Present tense
je sors
tu sors
il/elle sort
nous sortons
vous sortez
ils/elles sortent

obtenir (to obtain, to get)

Present tense
j'obtiens
tu obtiens
il/elle obtient
nous obtenons
vous obtenez
ils/elles obtiennent

Perfect tense
j'ai obtenu, etc.

Future tense
j'obtiendrai, etc.

CONVERSATION

L'anglais en trois mois

David   Est-ce que vous vous servez toujours du magnétophone que vous avez acheté récemment?

Isabelle   Non, je ne me sers plus de celui-là. Je m'en suis débarrassée et je me suis acheté un magnétophone portatif beaucoup plus perfectionné.

David   N'est-il pas difficile d'apprécier la musique avec une si petite machine?

Isabelle   Vous vous trompez, ce n'est pas de la musique que j'écoute, ce sont des cassettes d'anglais. Je les ai achetées parce que je dois apprendre l'anglais en trois mois.

David   Est-ce que vous avez le temps d'écouter ces cassettes?

Isabelle   Oui, bien sûr. Je les écoute le matin lorsque je me lave, lorsque je m'habille, lorsque je me peigne, lorsque je me maquille ... ce qui prend un certain temps. Mon mari écoute les cassettes aussi quand il se rase, quand il se lave et se brosse les dents. Le dimanche nous aimons sortir et j'écoute encore mes cassettes lorsque nous nous promenons au parc et lorsque nous nous asseyons sur un banc pour nous reposer.

David   Ce n'est pas une attitude très sociable.

Isabelle   C'est vrai, mais si je réussis à apprendre l'anglais en trois mois, il me sera possible d'obtenir une promotion et de voyager en Angleterre et aux États-Unis.

David   Bon, alors, bonne chance ou comme on dit en anglais 'good luck'!

TRANSLATION

English in three months

David   Are you still using the tape recorder you bought recently?

Isabelle No, I'm not using that one anymore. I've gotten rid of it and I've bought myself a much more sophisticated (*lit.* "perfected") portable tape recorder.

David   Isn't it difficult to appreciate music with such a small machine?

Isabelle You're mistaken, it's not music I listen to, it's English language cassettes (*lit.* "cassettes of English"). I bought them because I must learn English in three months.

David   Do you have the time to listen to these cassettes?

Isabelle Yes, of course. I listen to them in the morning when I'm washing, when I'm getting dressed, when I'm combing my hair, when I'm putting my makeup on ... which takes a certain amount of time (*lit.* "a certain time").
My husband also listens to the cassettes when he's shaving, when he's washing and brushing his teeth. On Sundays we like to go out and I listen to my cassettes again when we're walking in the park and when we sit down on a bench to rest.

David   That's not a very sociable attitude.

Isabelle That's true, but if I succeed in learning English in three months, it will be possible for me to get a promotion and to travel to England and the United States.

David   Good, well, good luck, or, as they say in English, "good luck!"

Chapter 11

Conjunctions – words like "because" and "while" that join parts of a sentence together – are discussed here, together with:

- *numbers over 100*
- *the passive voice*
- *the present participle*
- *more about the imperative form*
- *the pluperfect ("I had spoken," etc.)*
- *using "**depuis**" ("since") and "**venir de**" ("to have just … ")*

---

68 Conjunctions

Study the following:

Reason

parce que	because
car	for, because
puisque	since
comme	as, since
donc	so, therefore

Time

quand	when
lorsque	when
dès que	as soon as
aussitôt que	as soon as
pendant que	while
maintenant que	now that

Contrast

mais	but
tandis que	whereas

Other conjunctions will be discussed in the next chapter.

Examples:

Nous avons acheté une tente, car nous voulons faire du camping.
> We have bought a tent, because we want to go camping.

Ma mère n'aime pas les tentes, donc nous avons acheté une caravane.
> My mother doesn't like tents, so we've bought a trailer.

Puisque tu es fatigué, nous pourrions camper ici.
> Since you're tired, we could camp here.

Pendant que tu vas chercher de l'eau potable, je vais monter la tente.
> While you go and get some drinking water, I'll put up the tent.

C'est un bon camping, mais où sont les toilettes?
> It's a good campsite, but where are the bathrooms?

Note that you must use the future tense after **quand, lorsque, dès que**, and **aussitôt que** when the future is referred to:

Quand nous ferons du camping l'année prochaine, toute la famille s'amusera bien.
> When we go camping next year, the whole family will have a good time.

Aussitôt que tu auras monté la tente, je préparerai à manger.
> As soon as you have put up the tent, I'll prepare something to eat.

BUT not if "when" means "whenever":

Quand je suis en vacances, je dépense toujours beaucoup d'argent.
> When I'm on vacation, I always spend a lot of money.

Vocabulary

le lit de camp	cot (for camping)
le sac de couchage	sleeping bag
le champ	field
la piscine	swimming pool
supplémentaire	extra
tomber en panne	to break down

Exercise 57

Translate:

1 Since Paul's friend *(m.)* is coming camping with us, we'll have to buy an extra cot (for camping).
2 When you can speak French, we'll go camping in France.
3 Do you take every opportunity to speak French, when you're in Belgium?
4 I don't like this campsite because there's no swimming pool.
5 There are four of us (say "We are four") but we have only three sleeping bags.
6 The car broke down, so we decided to camp in a field.

69 Numerals over 100

Study the following:

100	cent	800	huit cents
101	cent un	960	neuf cent soixante
110	cent dix	1,000	mille
150	cent cinquante	1,250	mille deux cent cinquante
200	deux cents		
300	trois cents	2,000	deux mille
400	quatre cents	8,000	huit mille
520	cinq cent vingt	9,000	neuf mille
640	six cent quarante	1,000,000	un million
750	sept cent cinquante		

Note:

a) **cent** drops the s when followed by another number:
trois cents livres BUT **trois cent quarante livres**

b) when followed by a noun, **un million** takes **de:**
un million de francs

c) in dates **mille** is sometimes written **mil:**
en mille (or **mil**) **neuf cent quatre-vingt-seize**

Study the following ordinal numbers:

1st	**premier**	8th	**huitième**
2nd	**deuxième**	9th	**neuvième**
3rd	**troisième**	10th	**dixième**
4th	**quatrième**	20th	**vingtième**
5th	**cinquième**	21st	**vingt et unième**
6th	**sixième**	22nd	**vingt-deuxième**
7th	**septième**		

Note:

a) **premier** has a feminine form: **première**

b) **deuxième** has an alternative: **second, seconde** (*f.*)

c) the spelling of **cinquième** and **neuvième**

d) in French we don't say "Louis the Fourteenth," we say
"Louis fourteen," etc.: **Louis quatorze, Henri huit**

Exercise 58

Complete the following, writing the answers in full:

a) 150 + 100 =   d) 450 + 120 =
b) 260 + 40 =   e) 580 + 100 =
c) 320 + 110 =   f) 1000 + 440 =

Vocabulary

le casino	casino
le concert	concert
le ballet	ballet
l'opéra (m.)	opera
la discothèque	disco
la boîte de nuit	nightclub
la patinoire	skating rink

Exercise 59

Translate:

1 the first disco
2 the second casino
3 the third nightclub
4 the fourth theater
5 the fifth concert
6 the sixth opera
7 the seventh movie
8 the eighth skating rink
9 the ninth ballet
10 the tenth restaurant

70 The passive voice

The passive is formed, as in English, with the verb **être** and the past participle that agrees with the subject; "by" is translated **par**:

Un tunnel sera construit sous la Manche.
   A tunnel will be built under the English Channel.
Le traité a été signé par les deux gouvernements.
   The treaty has been signed by both governments.

"By" is sometimes translated **de**, especially after verbs of feeling:

La Reine est respectée de tout le monde.
The Queen is respected by everyone.

The French have a tendency to avoid the passive and do so in one of the following ways:

a) by using the pronoun on (see Chapter 10):

On a déjà oublié le tunnel que les Britanniques ont annulé en 1975.
The tunnel that the British canceled in 1975 has already been forgotten.

Be careful with those verbs that take an indirect object like **donner à** (to give to), **dire à** (to tell, to say to), **répondre à** (to reply to, to answer), **demander à** (to ask), because although we can say in English "I've been given," "he's been told," "the letter has been answered," "she's been asked," etc., this construction is impossible in French and you must use **on:**

On m'a dit qu'il y aura un train toutes les trois minutes.
I've been told that there will be a train every three minutes.
On lui a demandé ce qu'il pensait du projet.
He was asked what he thought of the project.
On a déjà répondu à la lettre.
The letter has already been answered.

b) by changing the roles of subject and agent and using the active voice:

La construction d'un lien fixe trans-Manche créera beaucoup d'emplois.
Many jobs will be created by the building of a cross-Channel fixed link.

c) by occasionally using a reflexive verb:

Cela ne se vend pas en France. That's not sold in France.

176

Vocabulary

le continent	continent
la traversée	crossing
la république	republic
la décision	decision
l'importance *(f.)*	importance
ferroviaire	rail
routier, routière *(f.)*	road
historique	historic
étranger, étrangère *(f.)*	foreign
relierv	to link
annoncer	to announce
souligner	to emphasize

Irregular verb:

construire
(to build)

Present tense

je construis
tu construis
il/elle construit
nous construisons
vous construisez
ils/elles construisent

Perfect tense

j'ai construit, etc.

Exercise 60

Change the following into the passive:

1 Le président de la République française a souligné l'importance de la décision.
2 Un tunnel ferroviaire reliera la Grande-Bretagne au continent en 1993.
3 On construira plus tard un lien routier.
4 On a annoncé cette décision historique à Lille.
5 La traversée de la Manche a souvent découragé les touristes étrangers.

71 The present participle

The present participle in English ends in -ing, and it is often preceded by "while," "on," "by," "in;" in French it ends in **-ant** and is often preceded by **en:**

Il s'est cassé la jambe, en jouant au football.
He broke his leg while playing soccer.
En étudiant un peu tous les jours, vous apprendrez le français en trois mois.
By studying a little every day, you will learn French in three months.

The present participle can be used, as in English, without a preceding preposition:

Voyant que le patron était de bonne humeur, il a demandé une augmentation de salaire.
Seeing that the boss was in a good mood, he asked for an increase in salary.

The present participle is formed by removing the -ons from the first person plural of the present tense and adding **-ant:**

chantant	singing
finissant	finishing
vendant	selling
écrivant	writing

There are three exceptions: **avoir**, **être**, and **savoir**:

ayant	having
étant	being
sachant	knowing

Remember that **en** is the only preposition that is followed by the present participle in French; all others are followed by the infinitive (see Chapter 10).

Remember also that sentences such as "I am going," "I am watching," "I am listening" are translated by the present tense (see Chapter 2):

je vais
je regarde
j'écoute

Vocabulary

le bras	arm
le cours	course, class
le diplôme	diploma
l'agent de police	police officer
la fois	time, occasion
la réponse	reply
blessé	injured
par	per
faire du ski	to ski
tomber	to fall (conjugated with **être**)
patiner	to skate
appeler	to call (see Chapter 12)

Irregular verb:

voir (to see)

Present tense
je vois
tu vois
il/elle voit
nous voyons
vous voyez
ils/elles voient

Perfect tense
j'ai vu, etc.

Future tense
je verrai, etc.

Exercise 61

Combine the following using a present participle:

1 Elle s'est cassé le bras. Elle faisait du ski.
2 Je suis tombé. Je patinais.
3 Il allait aux cours du soir trois fois par semaine. Il a obtenu son diplôme.
4 L'agent de police a vu que l'automobiliste était blessé. Il a appelé une ambulance.
5 Vous téléphonez. Vous aurez la réponse tout de suite.

72 More about the imperative

The imperative of **avoir** and **être** is:

aie	have *(fam.)*	**sois**	be *(fam.)*
ayez	have	**soyez**	be
ayons	let's have	**soyons**	let's be

Examples:

Ayez un peu de patience. Have a little patience.
Ne soyez pas en retard. Don't be late.
Soyons raisonnables. Let's be reasonable.

73 The imperative with pronouns

Study the following:

Invitez votre secrétaire au restaurant.
Invite your secretary to the restaurant.
Invitez-la. Invite her.
Ne l'invitez pas. Don't invite her.

Donnez le numéro de téléphone aux clients.
Give the telephone number to the clients.
Donnez-leur le numéro. Give them the number.
Ne leur donnez pas le numéro. Don't give them the
number.

Asseyez-vous dans ce fauteuil. Sit down in this armchair.
Ne vous asseyez pas dans ce fauteuil.
Don't sit down in this armchair.

You will have noticed that:

a) pronouns follow the verb in the affirmative imperative.
b) pronouns precede the verb in the negative imperative.

Study the following:

Donnez-moi votre adresse.
Donnez-la-moi.
Ne me donnez pas votre adresse.
Ne me la donnez pas.
Couche-toi.
Ne te couche pas.
You will have noticed that:

a) **me** and **te** become **moi and toi** in the affirmative imperative.
b) in the affirmative imperative we say **donnez-le-moi, envoyez-la-moi, montrez-les-moi.**

Remember, of course, that an imperative can be made more polite by putting one of the following expressions in front of the infinitive:

Voulez-vous … ?	Will you … ?
Voulez-vous bien … ?	Would you kindly … ?
Pourriez-vous … ?	Could you … ?

Examples:

Voulez-vous signer ici, s'il vous plaît?
    Will you sign here, please?
Voulez-vous bien passer à la caisse, s'il vous plaît?
    Would you kindly go to the register, please?
Pourriez-vous nous apporter encore du café?
    Could you bring us some more coffee?

Vocabulary

le catalogue	catalog
l'échantillon (*m.*)	sample
la brochure	brochure
faire des heures (*f.*) **supplémentaires**	to work overtime

74 The pluperfect

"I had called," "I had spoken," etc., is expressed by using the imperfect of **avoir** or **être** with the past participle:

J'avais déjà téléphoné à l'hôpital.
 I had already called the hospital.
Elle était déjà partie, quand son mari est arrivé.
 She had already left, when her husband arrived.

75 "Depuis" (since)

The French sometimes use the present tense where we use the past tense in English. This happens when an action, that began in the past is still continuing in the present:

Depuis quand êtes-vous en France?
> How long have you been in France? (lit. "Since when
> are you in France?")

Depuis combien de temps apprenez-vous le français?
> How long have you been learning French?

**Je suis en France depuis une semaine, mais j'apprends le
français depuis trois mois.**
> I've been in France for a week, but I've been learning
> French for three months.

76 "Venir de" (to have just ...)

This idiomatic expression, used only in the present and
imperfect tenses, expresses the idea of "having just done
something."

Je viens d'acheter une maison.
> I have just bought a house.

Elle venait de vendre son appartement.
> She had just sold her apartment.

Vocabulary

le docteur	doctor
le pompier	firefighter
l'ambulancier	ambulance driver
le permis de conduire	driver's license
jouer du piano	to play the piano
prévenir	to inform (conjugated like venir)
transporter	to transport

Exercise 63

Translate:

1 I've been married for five years.
2 I've lived in this house for four years.
3 I've worked for this bank for three years.
4 I've had this car for two years.
5 I've been learning to play the piano for one year.

Exercise 64

Answer the questions as follows:

Allez-vous téléphoner à la police?
    Are you going to call the police?
Mais je viens de téléphoner à la police.
    But I've just called the police.

1 Allez-vous appeler un docteur?
2 Allez-vous prévenir les pompiers?
3 Pouvez-vous me montrer votre permis de conduire?
4 Est-ce que les ambulanciers vont transporter les blessés à l'hôpital?
5 Est-ce que vous allez me donner votre adresse?

Vocabulary

le volant	steering wheel
le rêve	dream
le moment	moment
le projet	project
l'isolement *(m.)*	isolation
la nouvelle	news
la liaison	link
la fin	end
l'île *(f.)*	island
la façon	way
l'entente *(f.)*	understanding
nécessaire	necessary
contre	against
cordial	cordial
jurer	to swear
réaliser	to realize
vive	long live

Irregular verb:

vivre (to live)

Present tense

je vis
tu vis
il/elle vit
nous vivons
vous vivez
ils/elles vivent

Perfect tense

j'ai vécu, etc.

CONVERSATION

Le tunnel sous la Manche

Une conversation entre un Anglais et une Française

Anglais   On vient d'annoncer une grande nouvelle. La décision a été prise de construire un tunnel ferroviaire sous la Manche!

Française   Vraiment? Depuis le temps qu'on en parle! Un tunnel ferroviaire, vous dites? Mais le premier ministre britannique avait juré qu'elle serait la première à traverser la Manche au volant de sa voiture.

Anglais   Oui, c'est vrai, mais aussitôt que la liaison routière sera construite, elle pourra réaliser son rêve.

Française   À ce moment-là elle ne sera peut-être plus premier ministre! Qu'est-ce que vous pensez vous-même du projet?

Anglais   Eh bien, en prenant cette décision, on met fin à l'isolement de la Grande-Bretagne, ce qui est nécessaire si on veut vivre au vingtième siècle, et en même temps on créera de nouveaux emplois.

Française   Y a-t-il des gens qui sont contre le projet?

Anglais   Oui, il y a des gens qui pensent que la Grande-Bretagne devrait rester une île. Ils ont peut-être raison.

Française   Oui, peut-être, mais de toutes façons, avec un tunnel ou sans tunnel – vive l'Entente cordiale!

TRANSLATION

The Tunnel under the English Channel

A conversation between an Englishman and a Frenchwoman

Englishman   An important piece of news (*lit.* "a big news") has just been announced. The decision has been taken to build a rail tunnel under the Channel!

Frenchwoman   Really? They've been talking about it for a long time! (*lit.* "Since the time one is talking about it!"). A rail tunnel, you say? But the British Prime Minister swore (*lit.* "had sworn") that she would be the first to cross the Channel at the wheel of her car.

Englishman   Yes, it's true, but as soon as the road link is built (*lit.* "will be built"), she'll be able to realize her dream.

Frenchwoman   Then she may no longer be Prime Minister! What do you yourself think about the project?

Englishman   Well, by taking this decision, they are putting an end to Britain's isolation, which is necessary if we want to live in the twentieth century, and at the same time they are creating new jobs.

Frenchwoman   Are there people who are against the project?

Englishman   Yes, there are some people who think that Britain should remain an island. Perhaps they're right.

Frenchwoman   Yes, perhaps, but in any case (*lit.* "of all ways"), with a tunnel or without a tunnel – long live the Entente Cordiale!

Chapter 12

In this final chapter you will study the use of *"faire"* in its variety of meanings. Then move on to:

• the past historic tense in both regular and irregular verbs
• spelling changes in verbs (to keep them regular)
• verbs needing/not needing a preposition
• the subjunctive mood, used to express a wish or suggestion

77 The verb faire

Faire is the most overworked verb in the French language. It is conjugated as follows:

Present tense

je fais	**nous faisons**
tu fais	**vous faites**
il/elle fait	**ils/elles font**

Perfect tense
j'ai fait

Imperfect tense
je faisais

Future tense
je ferai

Faire can have a variety of meanings, as shown in the following examples.

a) to do:
Qu'est-ce que vous faites dans la vie?
    What do you do for a living?

b) to make:
Ma mère va faire un gâteau.
    My mother is going to make a cake.

c) to give:
Je vais faire une conférence sur la graphologie.
    I'm going to give a lecture on graphology.

d) to take:
Elle aime faire une promenade au parc.
    She likes to take a walk in the park.

e) to have:
Mon mari fait de la tension.
    My husband has high blood pressure.

f) to act:
Ne fais pas l'idiot.
    Don't play the fool.

g) to force:
Je l'ai fait travailler.
    I forced him to work (or I made him work).

h) to have something done:
Ils font construire une maison.
    They're having a house built.

i) it is used to talk about the weather (see Chapter 6):
Il fait beau.
    The weather is fine.

j) it is used in many idiomatic expressions:
Tu me fais marcher.
    You're pulling my leg.

Vocabulary

la profession	profession
la tarte	tart, pie
la pomme	apple
la psychologie	psychology
la fièvre	fever
bête	silly

Exercise 65

Rewrite the following using the verb faire:

1 Quelle est votre profession?
2 Ma soeur prépare une tarte aux pommes.
3 Je vais parler de la psychologie devant 200 personnes.
4 Elle s'est promenée au parc hier.
5 Il a de la fièvre.
6 Ne sois pas bête.
7 J'ai forcé mon fils à travailler.
8 On me construit une maison à Avignon.

78 The past historic

There is a past tense that you will meet when reading books, magazines, and newspapers, but almost never in conversation. This is called the past historic or past definite. It is a literary tense and you yourself will never need to use it, but you must be able to recognize it.

The past historic describes a completed action in the past and, in the case of regular verbs, is formed by removing the **-er, -ir, -re**, from the infinitive and adding the following endings:

-er verbs		-ir/-re verbs	
je	-ai	je	-is
tu	-as	tu	-is
il/elle	-a	il/elle	-it
nous	-âmes	nous	-îmes
vous	-âtes	vous	-îtes
ils/elles	-èrent	ils/elles	-irent

Examples:

Le lendemain Paul arriva tôt.
The following day Paul arrived early.
Les touristes visitèrent cinq pays en cinq jours.
The tourists visited five countries in five days.
Victor Hugo finit d'écrire Les Misérables en 1862.
Victor Hugo finished writing *Les Misérables* in 1862.

79 The past historic of irregular verbs

You will sometimes be able to recognize the past historic of irregular verbs by the similarity to the past participle:

Infinitive	Perfect tense	Past historic	Meaning
dire	j'ai dit	je dis	I said
mettre	j'ai mis	je mis	I put
prendre	j'ai pris	je pris	I took
sortir	je suis sorti	je sortis	I went out
avoir	j'ai eu	j'eus	I had
lire	j'ai lu	je lus	I read
vivre	j'ai vécu	je vécus	I lived

Other irregular forms just have to be learned:

Infinitive	Perfect tense	Past historic	Meaning
écrire	j'ai écrit	j'écrivis	I wrote
être	j'ai été	je fus	I was
faire	j'ai fait	je fis	I did
venir	je suis venu	je vins	I came
voir	j'ai vu	je vis	I saw

Exercise 66

Translate into English:

1 Il donna.
2 Je vendis.
3 Nous finîmes.
4 Elle eut.
5 Je fus.

6 Vous eûtes.
7 Il prit.
8 Elle sortit.
9 Ils lurent.
10 Elles mirent.

---

80 Verbs needing a preposition in English, but not in French, and vice versa

Although a preposition is necessary in English to complete the meaning of the following English verbs, none is required in French:

to approve of	**approuver**
to listen to	**écouter**
to look at	**regarder**
to look for	**chercher**
to ask for	**demander**
to pay for	**payer**
to wait for	**attendre**

Conversely, a preposition is sometimes needed in French but not in English:

demander à	to ask
dire à	to tell
défendre à	to forbid
obéir à	to obey
permettre à	to allow
ressembler à	to resemble
toucher à	to touch
jouer à	to play (game)
jouer de	to play (instrument)

Examples:

J'ai écouté les explications du guide avec attention.
I listened carefully to the guide's explanations.
Regardez la cathédrale à droite.
Look at the cathedral on the right.
Attendez les autres membres du groupe.
Wait for the other members of the group.
Nous cherchons les toilettes.
We are looking for the toilets.
Je vais demander deux billets d'entrée.
I'm going to ask for two admission tickets.
Il aime jouer au tennis.
He likes to play tennis.
Elle aime jouer du piano.
She likes to play the piano.

81 Spelling changes

In French, a verb can only be regarded as regular if its basic sound remains the same throughout the conjugation. In order to retain this basic sound, we sometimes have to make changes in the spelling. Let's take an example.

- We have learned that we form the present tense by removing the **-er** from the infinitive and adding certain endings, and in the case of **nous**, we add **-ons.** But if we do this with the verb **manger** (to eat), pronounced "mah*ng*-zhay," we will have "**mangons**," pronounced "mah*ng*-go*ng*;" i.e. a change in the basic sound. So, in order to keep the soft sound "zh," we must add an e, and we write **nous mangeons.** This spelling change takes place whenever the **g** is followed by **o** or **a**:

nous mangeons	we eat	(present tense)
je mangeais	I was eating	(imperfect)
il mangea	he ate	(past historic)
en mangeant	while eating	(present participle)

Here are some important verbs that behave like **manger**:

arranger	to arrange
corriger	to correct
décourager	to discourage
encourager	to encourage
déranger	to disturb
nager	to swim
voyager	to travel

- Everything that has been said about keeping the **g** soft also applies to the soft **c** in a verb like **annoncer** (to announce). In order to keep the **c** soft in the nous-form, we have to add a cedilla to the **c**, and we write **nous annonçons.** If we don't do this, the pronunciation will be "ah-no*ng*-ko*ng*." Therefore, we write **ç** before **o** and **a**:

nous annonçons	we announce
j'annonçais	I was announcing
il annonça	he announced
en annonçant	while announcing

Important verbs like **annoncer:**

commencer	to begin
divorcer	to divorce
prononcer	to pronounce
remplacer	to replace

- Some verbs whose infinitive ends in **-eler** and **-eter** double the **l** and **t** before a silent **e:**

  appeler (to call)

  Present tense

j'appelle	**nous appelons**
tu appelles	**vous appelez**
il/elle appelle	**ils/elles appellent**

  Future tense
  j'appellerai

  Conditional tense
  j'appellerais

  Important verbs like **appeler:**

rappeler	to call back, to remind
renouveler	to renew
jeter	to throw

- Some verbs change **e** to **è** before a silent **e:**

  acheter (to buy)

  Present tense

j'achète	**nous achetons**
tu achètes	**vous achetez**
il/elle achète	**ils/elles achètent**

Future tense
j'achèterai

Conditional tense
j'achèterais

Important verbs like **acheter:**

lever	to raise
se lever	to get up
mener	to lead
amener	to bring

- Some verbs change **é** to **è** before a silent **e** (present tense and present subjunctive only):

espérer (to hope)

Present tense

j'espère	**nous espérons**
tu espères	**vous espérez**
il/elle espère	**ils/elles espèrent**

Important verbs like **espérer:**

considérer	to consider
régler	to settle
répéter	to repeat
s'inquiéter	to worry
préférer	to prefer

Verbs whose infinitive ends in **-yer** change **y** to **i** before a silent **e:**

nettoyer (to clean)

Present tense

je nettoie	**nous nettoyons**
tu nettoies	**vous nettoyez**
il/elle nettoie	**ils/elles nettoient**

Future tense
je nettoierai

Conditional tense
je nettoierais

Important verbs like **nettoyer**:

employer	to use
s'ennuyer	to be bored
envoyer	to send (*Future:* **j'enverrai**)
payer	to pay (optional spelling change)
essayer	to try (optional spelling change)

82 The subjunctive

We have a subjunctive mood in English, although it is used much less often than in French. In English, when we make a suggestion or express a wish, we use the subjunctive. For example, when we say "I suggest that a vote be taken" or "I wish today were Saturday," "be" and "were" are subjunctives.

• In French, we use the subjunctive after verbs and expressions that denote:

a)	a wish	**vouloir, désirer**	to want, to wish
b)	a preference	**préférer**	to prefer
c)	a suggestion	**suggérer, proposer**	to suggest
d)	a necessity	**falloir**	to be necessary
e)	a demand	**exiger**	to demand
f)	surprise	**être surpris**	to be surprised
g)	regret	**regretter**	to regret
h)	anger	**être furieux**	to be furious
i)	fear	**avoir peur**	to be afraid
j)	doubt	**douter**	to doubt
k)	possibility	**être possible**	to be possible
l)	pleasure	**être content**	to be pleased
m)	sorrow	**être désolé**	to be sorry

- The subjunctive is always preceded by the conjunction **que** (that). It is formed by removing the **-ent** ending from the third person plural form of the present tense and adding:

je	-e	nous	-ions
tu	-es	vous	-iez
il/elle	-e	ils/elles	-ent

Examples:

... que je parle   ... que nous vendions
... que tu donnes   ... que vous répondiez
... qu'il finisse   ... qu'ils mettent
... qu'elle maigrisse   ... qu'elles permettent

- Examples of the use of the subjunctive:

Je voudrais que vous me fixiez un rendez-vous chez le coiffeur.
I would like you to fix an appointment for me at the hairdresser's.
Je voudrais que vous me coupiez les cheveux.
I would like you to cut my hair.
Je préfère qu'il ne me coupe pas les cheveux trop court.
I prefer he didn't cut my hair too short.
Je veux qu'il me rase.
I want him to shave me.
Il faut que vous me mettiez un peu de laque (*f.*) **sur les cheveux à cause du vent.**
You must put a little hairspray on my hair because of the wind.
Je suis surpris(e) que le coiffeur ne vende pas de peignes (*m.*).
I am surprised that the hairdresser doesn't sell combs.
Je suis content(e) que vous me parliez en français.
I am pleased that you are talking to me in French.

It is important to note that when the subject of the dependent verb is the same as that of the main verb, the construction with an infinitive is used. Compare:

Je voudrais partir. I'd like to leave.
Nous voudrions partir. We'd like to leave.

BUT

Nous voudrions que vous partiez. We'd like you to leave.

- There are some irregular subjunctives and the most important are:

être (to be)	**que je sois, il soit, nous soyons, ils soient**
avoir (to have)	**que j'aie, il ait, nous ayons, ils aient**
aller (to go)	**que j'aille, il aille, nous allions, ils aillent**
faire (to do,)	**que je fasse, il fasse, nous fassions, ils fassent**
pouvoir (to be able)	**que je puisse, il puisse, nous puissions, ils puissent**
prendre (to take)	**que je prenne, il prenne, nous prenions, ils prennent**
savoir (to know)	**que je sache, il sache, nous sachions, ils sachent**
venir (to come)	**que je vienne, il vienne, nous venions, ils viennent**

- The subjunctive is also used after the following conjunctions – those marked * require **ne** before the verb:

quoique	although
bien que	although
pour que	in order that
afin que	in order that
de peur que*	for fear that
à condition que	on condition that
pourvu que	provided that
jusqu'à ce que	until
à moins que*	unless
avant que*	before

200

Examples:

Bien qu'il sache parler français, il refuse de téléphoner à Paris.
> Although he can speak French, he refuses to call Paris.

J'ai acheté ce poste de radio pour que vous puissiez écouter les émissions françaises.
> I've bought this radio so that you can listen to French broadcasts.

Je veux bien vous donner les cassettes, à condition que vous étudiez chaque soir.
> I'm quite willing to give you the cassettes, on the condition that you study every evening.

A moins que vous ne m'aidiez, je ne pourrai pas finir cet exercice.
> Unless you help me, I won't be able to finish this exercise.

Je dois rester ici jusqu'à ce que ma femme arrive.
> I must stay here until my wife arrives.

- The subjunctive is also used after:

a) a superlative:

C'est la plus grande librairie que nous ayons jamais vue.
> This is the biggest bookstore we have ever seen.

b) **seul** (only), **premier** (first), **dernier** (last):

Paul est le seul qui puisse aller à la réunion.
> Paul is the only one who can go to the meeting.

c) an indefinite antecedent:

Je cherche un médecin qui sache parler anglais.
> I'm looking for a doctor who can speak English.
> (*i.e.* I'm not sure that one exists)

BUT

Je cherche le médecin qui sait parler anglais.
I'm looking for the doctor who can speak English.
(*i.e.* I know he exists)

d) impersonal verbs such as:

Il faut que ...	It is necessary that ...
Il vaut mieux que ...	It is better that ...
Il est important que ...	It is important that ...
Il est possible que ...	It is possible that ...
Il est inévitable que ...	It is inevitable that ...
Il est dommage que ...	It is a pity that ...

Examples:

Il est important que nous réservions les chambres à l'avance.
It is important that we reserve the rooms in advance.
Il est dommage qu'il ne vienne pas aujourd'hui.
It is a pity that he's not coming today.

e) the negative of **penser** (to think) and **croire** (to believe). Compare:

Je pense que Caroline va à la réception.
I think that Caroline is going to the reception.
Je ne pense pas que Caroline aille à la réception.
I don't think Caroline is going to the reception.

f) **quoi que** (whatever):

... quoi que vous fassiez ...
... whatever you do ...

g) **quel que, quelle que, quels que, quelles que** (whatever):

... quelle que soit la raison ...
... whatever the reason may be ...

- The subjunctive is also used for the third person imperative:

Qu'il prenne le parapluie. Let him take the umbrella.
Qu'elle parte. Let her leave.
Qu'ils fassent la vaisselle. Let them do the washing up.

- Note that there is also a perfect subjunctive that is used for action in the past. The perfect subjunctive is formed with **avoir** or **être:**

Je suis content que vous ayez retrouvé votre portefeuille.
   I am pleased that you have found your wallet.
Je suis désolé qu'elle soit tombée malade.
   I am sorry that she has fallen ill.

Vocabulary

le lancement	launching
le vaisseau spatial	spacecraft
le discours	speech
l'espace (m.)	space
la déclaration	statement
la conquête	conquest
la mission	mission
l'apesanteur (f.)	weightlessness
l'expérience (f.)	experiment, experience
les données (f.)	data
continuer	to continue
participer	to take part
filmer	to film
enregistrer	to record
reporter	to postpone
mener	to conduct
avoir lieu	to take place
en direct	live
quand même	still, nevertheless

Exercise 67

Translate:

1 I suggest that the president make a statement on television.
2 We must continue our conquest of space.
3 He would like the launching of the spacecraft to take place next week.
4 I am pleased that you are taking part in this space mission.
5 It is important that the launching should be filmed live.
6 Unless you can give me all the data recorded by the computers, I cannot take a decision.
7 We are pleased that the president has decided to postpone his speech.
8 Although the astronauts are used to weightlessness, they still have a little difficulty carrying out their experiments on board the spacecraft.

Vocabulary

le/la graphologue	graphologist
le mariage	wedding, marriage
le(s) renseignement(s) *(m.)*	information
l'échantillon *(m.)*	sample
la conversation téléphonique	telephone conversation
la personnalité	personality
la conclusion	conclusion
l'écriture *(f.)*	handwriting
l'analyse *(f.)*	analysis
les félicitations *(f.)*	congratulations
analyser	analyze
rédiger	to write, to compose
retarder	to delay
tout à fait	quite, completely
compatible	compatible
ordinaire	ordinary
favorable	favorable
alors	so
allô	hello (on the telephone)

CONVERSATION

Une conversation téléphonique entre un graphologue et une jeune cliente

Cliente	Allô. Bonjour, Monsieur. C'est vous le graphologue?
Graphologue	Oui, c'est moi.
Cliente	Eh bien, mon fiancé vient de fixer la date de notre mariage et ...
Graphologue	Félicitations, Mademoiselle!
Cliente	Merci. Je ne crois pas que je sois tout à fait prête pour le mariage, alors je voudrais que vous analysiez mon écriture et aussi celle de mon fiancé pour voir si nos personnalités sont compatibles.
Graphologue	Oui, c'est très facile. Il faut que vous m'envoyiez un échantillon de votre écriture et de celle de votre fiancé.
Cliente	Quelle sorte d'échantillon faut-il que je vous envoie?
Graphologue	Je préfère que vous écriviez une lettre tout à fait ordinaire, mais il faut qu'elle soit signée.
Cliente	Je doute que mon fiancé soit prêt à rédiger une lettre et à la signer sans savoir pourquoi.
Graphologue	Mais il est très important qu'il n'en connaisse pas la raison.
Cliente	Bon, très bien. Pour que vous puissiez arriver à une conclusion plus rapidement, est-ce qu'il faut que nous vous donnions des renseignements supplémentaires?
Graphologue	Non, pas du tout.
Cliente	Vous savez, cette analyse est très importante pour moi. A moins que votre rapport ne soit favorable, il est possible que je retarde le mariage.

TRANSLATION

A telephone conversation between a graphologist and a young client

Client	Hello. Good morning. Are you the graphologist?
Graphologist	Yes, I am.
Client	Well, my fiancé has just set the date of our wedding and ...
Graphologist	Congratulations!
Client	Thank you. I don't think I'm quite ready for marriage, so I would like you to analyze my handwriting and also my fiancé's in order to see if our personalities are compatible.
Graphologist	Yes, that's very easy. You must send me a sample of your handwriting and your fiancé's.
Client	What sort of sample must I send you?
Graphologist	I prefer you to write a perfectly ordinary letter, but it must be signed.
Client	I doubt whether my fiancé will be willing to write a letter and to sign it without knowing why.
Graphologist	But it's very important that he doesn't know the reason for it.
Client	OK, fine. So that you can come to a conclusion more rapidly, must we give you any additional information?
Graphologist	No, not at all.
Client	You know, this analysis is very important for me. Unless your report is favorable, it's possible that I may delay the wedding.

The following four exercises are not an essential part of the "Three Months" course, but you will certainly consolidate your knowledge of French if you make the effort to complete them. Do the Self-Assessment Test 3 first.

Exercise 68

Translate back into French all the English translations of the CONVERSATIONS that have appeared in this book.

Exercise 69

Translate back into French all the English translations of the EXAMPLES that have appeared in this book.

Exercise 70

Translate back into French all the English translations of the VOCABULARY LISTS that have appeared in this book.

Exercise 71

Translate back into English all the sentences in the KEY TO EXERCISES.

Self-Assessment Test 3

This Self-Assessment Test, based on Lessons 9-12, allows you to check on your progress and see whether any revision is needed. Deduct one point for every grammatical mistake or misspelling. The answers and score assessment are in the Key.

A: Reflexive verbs   Total: 11 points

Give the French for these sentences describing daily routines and what happened yesterday:

1 I wake up at 8 A.M.
2 I wash.
3 I shave.
4 I go to work.
5 Monique gets up at 9:00.
6 She washes.
7 She dresses quickly.
8 She goes to the office.
9 Nicole and I (f.) woke up at 10:00.
10 We put on our makeup.
11 We went to the station.

B: Verbs preceded by prepositions   Total: 4 points

Complete the following:

1 Il est parti [without saying] un mot.
2 Elle a hésité [before replying].
3 J'ai commencé [by criticizing] l'interprète.
4 [After having bought] un ordinateur, il a travaillé plus vite.

C: Conjunctions Total: 5 points

Complete the following sentences with the most suitable conjunction:

1 Nous avons acheté une tente, ____ nous voulons faire du camping.
2 Ma mère n'aime pas les tentes, ____ nous avons acheté une caravane.
3 ____ tu vas chercher de l'eau, je vais monter la tente.
4 C'est un bon camping, ____ où sont les toilettes?
5 ____ vous serez prêts, je préparerai à manger.

D: Numerals Total: 12 points

Complete the following, writing the totals in words:

a) 320 + 120   d) 260 + 50
b) 150 + 150   e) 1000 + 330
c) 580 + 200   f) 450 + 50

E: Peculiarities of French construction Total: 10 points

Give the French for:

1 How long have you been in America? (Use "tu")
2 I've been working here since the May 2nd.
3 We've been learning French for three months.
4 We've just bought an apartment.
5 They've just called a doctor.

F: Translation of "to" before an infinitive Total: 6 points

Complete the following:

1 [We hope to] aller à la plage.
2 [They've decided to] louer une voiture.
3 [They (f.) are pleased to] voir le soleil.
4 [She intends to] acheter des lunettes de soleil.
5 [I hesitate to] faire du ski nautique.
6 [Will you (tu) have the opportunity to] faire de la planche à voile?

G: The verb "faire" Total: 4 points

*Rewrite the following, using **faire:***

1 Quelle est votre profession?
2 Ma mère prépare un gâteau.
3 Je vais parler de la conquête de l'espace devant 100 personnes.
4 Il s'est promené au parc.

H: The imperative (with pronouns) Total: 16 points

Make up your mind! Give the French for:

1 (the letter) Copy it – no, don't copy it.
2 (the samples) Send them – no, don't send them.
3 (the catalog) Give it to me – no, don't give it to me.
4 Call them – no, don't call them.

I: The subjunctive Total: 8 points

Complete the following:

1 Je voudrais que [you fix] un rendez-vous.
2 Je veux bien vous aider, à condition que [you finish] le travail aujourd'hui.
3 Il est dommage que [Sophie isn't coming] à la réception.
4 Nous sommes contents que [they've found] une petite maison.

J: Conversation (Role-play) Total: 24 points

Take the part of Nicole:

Paul: Est-ce que tu écoutes toujours les cassettes que tu as achetées récemment?
Nicole: Yes, of course. I bought them because I have to learn English in three months.
Paul: Est-ce que tu as le temps d'écouter ces cassettes?
Nicole: Yes. If I listen to them in the morning when I'm washing. My husband listens to them as well, when he's shaving. If I succeed in learning English, it'll be possible for me to get a promotion and travel to the United States.

Reading Practice

These extracts from French literature and modern journals each have an English translation on the facing page. Refer to this as little as possible during your first reading of the French, then go through the piece again, noting constructions and vocabulary.

Les Misérables

L'hôpital était une maison étroite et basse à un seul étage avec un petit jardin.

Trois jours après son arrivée, l'évêque visita l'hôpital. La visite terminée, il fit prier le directeur de vouloir bien venir jusque chez lui.

– Monsieur le directeur de l'hôpital, lui dit-il, combien en ce moment avez-vous de malades?

– Vingt-six, monseigneur.

– C'est ce que j'avais compté, dit l'évêque.

– Les lits, reprit le directeur, sont bien serrés les uns contre les autres.

– C'est ce que j'avais remarqué.

– Les salles ne sont que des chambres et l'air s'y renouvelle difficilement.

– C'est ce qui me semble.

– Et puis, quand il y a un rayon de soleil, le jardin est bien petit pour les convalescents.

– C'est bien ce que je me disais.

Les Misérables

The hospital was a narrow and low two-story house with a small yard.

Three days after his arrival, the bishop visited the hospital. When the visit was over, he asked the director to be good enough to come home with him.

"Director," he said to him, "how many patients do you have at this moment?"

"Twenty-six, Monseigneur."

"That's how many I counted," said the bishop.

"The beds," continued the director, "are very close to each other."

"I noticed."

"The wards are only bedrooms and the air is not very fresh."

"I can imagine."

"And when we do get some sunshine, the yard is very small for the convalescents."

"That's what I was thinking."

– Dans les épidémies, nous avons eu cette année le typhus, nous avons eu la suette militaire il y a deux ans; cent malades quelquefois, nous ne savons que faire.

– C'est la pensée qui m'était venue.

– Que voulez-vous, monseigneur? dit le directeur, il faut se résigner.

Cette conversation avait lieu dans la salle à manger-galerie du rez-de-chaussée.

L'évêque garda un moment de silence, puis il se tourna brusquement vers le directeur de l'hôpital.

– Monsieur, dit-il, combien pensez-vous qu'il tiendrait de lits rien que dans cette salle?

– Dans la salle à manger de monseigneur? s'écria le directeur stupéfait.

L'évêque parcourait la salle du regard et semblait y faire avec les yeux des mesures et des calculs.

– Il y tiendrait bien vingt lits ! dit-il, comme se parlant à lui-même, puis élevant la voix:

– Tenez, monsieur le directeur de l'hôpital, je vais vous dire. Il y a évidemment une erreur. Vous êtes vingt-six personnes dans cinq ou six petites chambres. Nous sommes trois ici et nous avons place pour soixante, il y a erreur, je vous dis, vous avez mon logis et j'ai le vôtre. Rendez-moi ma maison; c'est ici chez vous.

Le lendemain les vingt-six pauvres malades étaient installés dans le palais de l'évêque et l'évêque était à l'hôpital.

Taken from Book 1, Chapter 2

Victor Hugo (1802-1885)

"When we have an epidemic, this year we've had typhus and two years ago we had military fever, with up to a hundred patients sometimes, we don't know what to do."

"That thought had occurred to me."

"What can one do, Monseigneur?" said the director. "We must resign ourselves to it."

This conversation took place in the ground floor banquet-hall.

The bishop remained silent for a moment, then he suddenly turned towards the director of the hospital.

"Tell me," he said, "how many beds do you think this room would hold?"

"The Monseigneur's dining room?" the director cried out, astonished.

The bishop looked around the room and seemed to be taking measurements and making calculations with his eyes.

"It would certainly hold twenty beds," he said, as if talking to himself. Then he raised his voice:

"Listen, Director, I'm going to tell you something. There's obviously an error. You have twenty-six people in five or six small bedrooms. There are three of us here and we have room for sixty. There's an error, I tell you. You have my house and I have yours. Give me back my house. You should be here. "

The following day the twenty-six poor patients were installed in the bishop's palace and the bishop was installed in the hospital.

214

France–Angleterre en une demi-heure

Paris à trois heures de Londres par le T.G.V.
Le premier ministre britannique et le président de la
République française ont choisi: la France et l'Angleterre
seront reliées, en 1993, par un tunnel ferroviaire à deux
tubes, assorti d'une galerie de service. Les véhicules, pour
traverser la Manche, devront donc prendre place sur des
navettes. Mme Thatcher, semble-t-il, aurait préféré, à côté
d'un tunnel pour les trains, un lien routier autonome.
C'est donc le projet du consortium franco-britannique
France-Manche/Channel Tunnel Group qui a été retenu.
Cependant, les deux gouvernements ont demandé à ses
responsables de déposer un projet de liaison routière destiné
à compléter l'ensemble ferroviaire d'ici à quinze ans. Faute
de présenter un tel projet, l'exclusivité de la concession
accordée sera perdue, a dit François Mitterrand.
Le 12 février, à Londres, sera signée la convention entre les
deux États. Après ratification par les Parlements d'ici à un
an, les travaux pourraient commencer à la mi- 1987 pour
une mise en service en 1993. Coût total de l'ouvrage: 53
milliards de francs.
Les navettes partiront toutes les trois minutes en période de
pointe. Trafic possible: quatre mille voitures par heure dans
chaque sens. La durée du parcours, long de quelque 50
kilomètres, sera de vingt-six minutes à une vitesse maximale
de 160 km/h. Il ne s'agit là bien sûr que de la traversée du
tunnel lui-même. La durée totale du trajet ferroviaire
Paris–Londres sera de quatre heures trente minutes en 1993;
de trois heures quand le T.G.V. sera en service.
Trafic voyageurs prévu en l'an 2000 entre les deux pays:
quarante-cinq millions de passagers répartis entre tous les
moyens de transport.

From Le Figaro 21.1.1986

Tunnel under the English Channel in 1993

France–England in half an hour

Paris – three hours from London by high-speed train.
The British Prime Minister and the President of the French
Republic have made their choice: France and England will
be linked, in 1993, by a twin-tunnel, equipped with a service
tunnel. Vehicles will therefore have to be placed on shuttle
trains for the Channel crossing. Mrs. Thatcher, apparently,
would have preferred an independent road link alongside
the rail tunnel.

So, it is the project submitted by the Franco-British
consortium France-Manche/Channel Tunnel Group that
has been accepted. However, both governments have asked
the consortium's management to submit a proposal for a
road link to complete the complex within fifteen years. If it
fails to submit such a proposal, the exclusive rights granted
will be lost, said François Mitterrand.

This agreement between the two countries will be signed
on February 12th in London. After ratification by the
Parliaments within a year, work could begin mid-1987 and
the scheme could be in operation in 1993. Total cost of the
work will be 53 thousand-million francs.

The shuttles will leave every three minutes at peak
periods. Potential traffic is four thousand cars per hour in
each direction. The duration of the journey, some 31 miles,
will be 26 minutes at a maximum speed of 100 miles per
hour. Of course, this refers only to the passage through the
tunnel itself. The total duration of the rail journey
Paris–London will be four hours and thirty minutes in 1993,
and three hours when the high-speed train is in service.

Passenger traffic expected in the year 2000 between the
two countries is forty-five million divided among all the
means of transport.

Papa, l'ordinateur et moi

On connaît enfin le profil de l'Homo informaticus moyen. C'est un petit garçon qui s'est fait offrir pour Noël un micro-ordinateur à bas prix et qui y pianote cinquante minutes par jour, six jours par mois, pour lutter contre des météorites en folie. Telles sont en substance les conclusions auxquelles ont abouti les enquêteurs de la Fnac* en sondant leurs clients.

Les chiffres révélés la semaine dernière parlent d'eux-mêmes. Scénario modèle: papa (90% des acheteurs sont des hommes), influencé par ses copains, se décide à offrir un micro-ordinateur à son rejeton. Papa est en général un cadre au niveau d'instruction universitaire. Il hésite peu, ne l'essaie pas et prend en général le moins cher (le prix est pour 67% des gens le premier critère de choix, avant même le nombre de logiciels disponibles et la facilité d'utilisation). Dès qu'il arrive à la maison, papa lit la notice et annonce à tout le monde qu'il a bien I 'intention de s'attaquer au basic (47% des acheteurs veulent apprendre à programmer avant l'achat). Mais cette belle ardeur est de courte durée. Papa n'a pas que ça à faire, et les manuels se montrent revêches. Il renonce. Les enfants prennent alors l'ordinateur en main (60% des utilisateurs ont moins de 25 ans, et parmi eux plus de la moitié ont moins de 15 ans). Ils veulent surtout s'amuser avec les logiciels qu'ils ont déjà vus dans les salles de jeux ou chez des amis. (Les programmes ludiques forment 55% des programmes vendus alors que les programmes utilitaires n'en composent que 12%). Ils piratent des cassettes ou des disquettes chez les copains (57%), inventent leurs propres programmes (71%), achètent de nouveaux logiciels (81%). Cependant, au bout de trois mois, le clavier plastique et le petit téléviseur ont perdu de leur magie. Les parents coriaces, qui étaient restés dans le coup jusque-là, finissent par abandonner, ne laissant qu'un noyau de fidèles irréductibles.

Enfin, toujours selon cette enquête chiffrée, l'ordinateur en s'immisçant dans nos foyers en bouleverserait l'ambiance. Il serait le champion du rapprochement des générations (estiment 55% d'utilisateurs) et (pour 18% de sondés) un sacré semeur de zizanie entre mari et femme …

By Bernard Werber, writing in Le Nouvel Observateur, December 1985. © LE NOUVEL OBSERVATEUR.

* Fédération nationale d'achats des cadres

Dad, the computer, and me

The profile of the average Homo informaticus is at last known. It is a small boy who has asked to be given an inexpensive micro-computer for Christmas and who taps away at it for fifty minutes a day, six days a month, in order to fight against crazed meteorites. These are, in substance, the conclusions reached by Fnac researchers who carried out a survey among their customers.

The figures revealed last week speak for themselves. Typical scenario: Dad (90% of purchasers are men), influenced by his pals, decides to buy a microcomputer for his offspring. Dad is usually an executive with a university education. He barely hesitates, doesn't try it out, and generally takes the least expensive one (for 67% of people the price is the most important criterion for choosing a computer, more important even than the amount of software available or ease of use). As soon as he arrives home, Dad reads the instructions and announces to everyone that he has every intention of tackling BASIC (47% of purchasers want to learn to program before buying). But this great enthusiasm is of short duration. Dad has other things to do, and the handbooks turn out to be rather daunting. He gives up.

The children then take over the computer (60% of users are aged under 25 and, of these, more than half are under 15). They particularly want to play with the software they have already seen in the amusement arcades or at friends' houses. (Computer games form 55% of all programs sold, while programs with a practical application account for only 12%). They pirate cassettes or diskettes at their friends' (57%), create their own programs (71%), buy new software (81%).

However, three months later, the plastic keyboard and the small television set have lost some of their magic. Persevering parents, who had participated in everything until then, finally give up, leaving just a small group of devoted enthusiasts.

Finally, again according to the statistics of this survey, it would seem that the computer, by intruding into our homes, upsets the atmosphere. Apparently, it is ideal for bringing the generations closer together (according to 55% of users) and (according to 18% of those interviewed) it is a constant source of friction (lit. "a right sower of discord") between husband and wife ...

Key to Exercises and Self-Assessment Tests

CHAPTER 1

Exercise 1: 1 le passeport. 2 l'hôtel. 3 la valise.
4 une station. 5 un magnétophone. 6 un chéquier.
7 une personne. 8 les journalistes. 9 les prix. 10 de la bière.
11 du vin. 12 des cassettes. 13 des journaux. 14 des autobus.

Exercise 2: 1 Oui, elle a un journal. 2 Oui, ils ont une
voiture. 3 Oui, j'ai une radio. 4 Oui, j'ai une carte.
5 Oui, nous avons une clé. 6 Oui, vous avez un disque.

Exercise 3: 1 Non, je n'ai pas de valise. 2 Non, je n'ai pas de
passeport. 3 Non, nous n'avons pas de vin. 4 Non, nous
n'avons pas de livre. 5 Non, il n'a pas de disques.
6 Non, elle n'a pas de radio. 7 Non, vous n'avez pas de
journaux. 8 Non, elles n'ont pas d'appareil-photo.

Exercise 4: 1 J'ai un magnétophone. 2 Je n'ai pas de clés.
3 Nous avons une valise. 4 Elle a de l'alcool. 5 Il n'a pas de
journal. 6 Ils ont des cassettes. 7 Elles n'ont pas de cartes.
8 Vous n'avez pas de chéquier. 9 Vous avez un appareil-
photo? 10 Vous avez des disques? 11 Vous avez des livres?
12 Vous avez une radio?

CHAPTER 2

Exercise 5: 1 Je suis médecin. 2 Il est pilote. 3 Elle est
journaliste. 4 Nous sommes banquiers. 5 Vous êtes avocat.
6 Elles sont hôtesses de l'air. 7 Ils sont astronautes.

Exercise 6: 1 Le banquier est pauvre. 2 La secrétaire est
stupide. 3 Les médecins sont malheureux. 4 Les journaux
sont ennuyeux. 5 Le vin est mauvais. 6 Le livre est difficile.
7 L'hôtesse de l'air est impolie. 8 La bière est bonne.

Exercise 7: 1 Nous habitons à Versailles. 2 Elle travaille à
Nice. 3 Il voyage. 4 Je parle deux langues. 5 Elles pratiquent

un sport. 6 Ils regardent la télévision. 7 Vous écoutez la radio. 8 Nous préparons une enquête.

Exercise 8: 1 Est-ce que vous téléphonez à l'hôtel? 2 Est-ce que vous réservez une chambre? 3 Est-ce que vous invitez le directeur à dîner? 4 Elle est intelligente? 5 Elle est intéressante? 6 Elle est grande? 7 Exporte-t-il des ordinateurs en France? 8 Importe-t-il des voitures? 9 Vote-t-il pour le président?

Exercise 9: a) neuf. b) deux. c) douze. d) cinq. e) quinze. f) douze. g) quatorze. h) trois. 1 Il y a sept jours dans la semaine. 2 James Bond, agent secret zéro zéro sept. 3 La date de la prise de la Bastille: le quatorze juillet. 4 Les Trois Mousquetaires sont finalement quatre. 5 Il y a douze mois dans l'année.

CHAPTER 3

Exercise 10: 1 Je finis le rapport. 2 Nous garantissons le magnétoscope. 3 Elle choisit un gâteau. 4 Il grossit. 5 Elles maigrissent. 6 Ils remplissent les verres. 7 Nous saisissons l'occasion.

Exercise 11: 1 Ce train est rapide. 2 Cette gare est importante. 3 Ce guichet est fermé. 4 Cette voiture est chère. 5 Cet ascenseur est plein. 6 Ces places sont réservées. 7 Ces compartiments sont occupés. 8 Ces billets sont valables.

Exercise 12: 1 J'ai soif. 2 Il a tort. 3 Elle a froid. 4 Nous avons faim. 5 Ils ont raison. 6 Elles ont chaud.

Exercise 13: 1 Non, je ne travaille pas. 2 Non, je n'écoute pas. 3 Non, je n'ai pas faim. 4 Nón, je ne choisis jamais de fromage. 5 Non, je ne téléphone jamais. 6 Non, je n'ai jamais froid. 7 Non, il ne mange rien. 8 Non, elle ne prépare rien. 9 Non, il n'exporte rien. 10 Non, nous n'invitons personne. 11 Non, nous ne choisissons personne. 12 Non, nous ne rencontrons personne. 13 Non, ils n'ont plus de voiture. 14 Non, elles n'habitent plus à Paris. 15 Non, elles ne travaillent plus.

Exercise 14: 1 Où travaillez-vous? 2 Quand regardez-vous le film? 3 Comment allez-vous? 4 Qui téléphone? 5 Qui cherchent-ils? 6 Pourquoi mangez-vous? 7 Quelles langues parlez-vous? 8 Combien de cassettes avez-vous? 9 Combien coûte ce journal? 10 Qu'est-ce que vous exportez? **Exercise 15:** 1 Réservez deux chambres. 2 Cherchez François. 3 Saisissez l'occasion. 4 Choisissez la méthode Hugo. 5 Montez les bagages. 6 Ne mangez pas trop. 7 Ne grossissez pas. 8 Ne fumez pas. 9 Parlons français. 10 Écoutons la radio. 11 Finissons le rapport.

CHAPTER 4

Exercise 16: 1 J'ai habité en France. 2 J'ai travaillé en Italie. 3 J'ai réservé les chambres. 4 Elle a écouté la radio. 5 Elle a regardé la télévision. 6 Elle a préparé le rapport. 7 Il a grossi. 8 Il a choisi le fromage. 9 Il a fini le livre. 10 Nous avons copié le document. 11 Nous avons acheté la voiture. 12 Nous avons téléphoné. 13 Vous avez garanti le magnétophone. 14 Vous avez saisi l'occasion. 15 Vous avez invité le président. 16 Ils ont maigri. 17 Elles ont dépensé 15 francs. 18 Elles ont traversé la Manche.

Exercise 17: 1 Non, je n'ai pas réservé la chambre. 2 Non, je n'ai pas écouté le disque. 3 Non, il n'a pas regardé le film. 4 Non, elle n'a pas préparé le document. 5 Non, nous n'avons pas fini. 6 Non, ils n'ont pas choisi. 7 Non, elles n'ont pas mangé.

Exercise 18: 1 Votre premier vol. 2 Attachez votre ceinture de sécurité. 3 Où sont nos billets? 4 Voici son passeport. 5 Voici sa place. 6 Leurs valises sont dans l'avion. 7 Notre horaire est important. 8 Où sont mes journaux?

Exercise 19: 1 C'est ennuyeux. 2 C'est mauvais. 3 C'est impossible. 4 C'est difficile. 5 C'est affreux. 6 C'est tôt.

Exercise 20: 1 Il est deux heures et quart. 2 Il est quatre heures et demie. 3 Il est six heures. 4 Il est huit heures vingt. 5 Le train arrive à dix heures et quart. 6 Le car arrive à midi moins le quart (or minuit moins le quart). 7 Le bateau part à midi vingt-cinq. 8 L'aéroglisseur part à une heure moins le quart. 9 Le président arrive à neuf heures et quart. 10 La conférence de presse est à dix heures et quart.

Exercise 21: 1 Le premier janvier. 2 Le quatorze février. 3 Le vingt et un mars. 4 Le premier avril. 5 Le dix-sept mars. 6 Le six juin. 7 Le quatorze juillet. 8 Le trente et un octobre. 9 Le vingt-trois septembre. 10 Le vingt-cinq octobre/ le sept novembre. 11 Le quatre juillet. 12 Le vingt-cinq décembre.

Exercise 22: 1 J'ai travaillé lundi. 2 J'ai écouté la radio mardi. 3 J'ai regardé la télévision mercredi. 4 J'ai fini le rapport jeudi. 5 J'ai acheté un disque vendredi. 6 J'ai téléphoné à ma femme samedi. 7 J'ai parlé espagnol dimanche. 8 Je travaille le lundi. 9 Elle écoute la radio le mardi. 10 Nous regardons la télévision le mercredi.

SELF-ASSESSMENT TEST 1

A: 1 le médecin. 2 l'ordinateur. 3 du vin. 4 de la bière. 5 ma voiture. 6 mes clés. 7 ce train. 8 ces journaux.

B: 1 riche. 2 heureux. 3 ennuyeux. 4 affreux. 5 difficile.

C: 1 regarder. 2 écouter. 3 choisir. 4 pratiquer. 5 fumer. 6 réserver. 7 voyager. 8 saisir. 9 consulter. 10 traverser.

D: 1 six heures et quart. 2 neuf heures moins le quart. 3 dix heures vingt. 4 midi/minuit moins le quart.

E: 1 mercredi. 2 dimanche. 3 vendredi. 4 mardi.

F: Jeudi means "on Thursday;" le jeudi means "on Thursdays," "every Thursday."

G: 1 le deux février. 2 le cinq avril. 3 le douze juin. 4 le trente et un août.

H: 1 Non, j'ai réservé les chambres lundi. 2 Non, il a fini le livre lundi. 3 Non, elle a copié le document lundi. 4 Non, ils ont téléphoné lundi.

I: 1 Je n'ai pas fini le rapport. 2 Elle n'a pas téléphoné à son mari samedi. 3 Nous n'avons pas visité l'Italie. 4 Ils n'ont pas maigri.

J: a) vingt-neuf. b) trente-six. c) quarante-cinq. d) trente et un. e) quarante-quatre. f) cinquante. g) quinze. h) soixante-deux. i) seize.

K: avoir

L: • Nous désirons passer deux semaines en France au printemps. Nous avons visité l'Italie en août, mais nous avons trouvé la chaleur insupportable. • Non, en voiture, c'est moins cher. • Oui, oui, oui. Je n'ai pas l'intention de traverser la Manche à la nage.

Score: 80%-100% = excellent. 60%-79% = good/very good. Progressing well. 45%-59% = satisfactory – but you should devote more time to your studies. Below 45% = serious review needed.

CHAPTER 5

Exercise 23: 1 Je vends ma voiture. 2 Il attend sa femme. 3 Nous rendons soixante francs. 4 Cela dépend de mes parents. 5 Est-ce qu'elles entendent la musique? 6 Elle a vendu sa maison. 7 Nous n'avons pas répondu. 8 Avez-vous descendu les bagages? 9 Attends-tu ton frère? 10 As-tu perdu ta mère?

Exercise 24: 1 Est-ce que vous avez pris le train? 2 J'ai appris le français. 3 Apprenez-vous la langue? 4 Comprenez-vous? 5 Tu as souvent surpris ton professeur?

Exercise 25: 1 J'ai mis une annonce dans le journal. 2 Il a permis à sa secrétaire de partir tôt. 3 Vous avez promis de répondre à la lettre? 4 Elle a soumis le rapport ce matin. 5 Mettez-vous le dictionnaire dans la valise? 6 Permettent-ils à leurs enfants de rentrer tard? 7 Nous promettons de parler français. 8 Soumettez-vous déjà le projet?

Exercise 26: 1 rapidement. 2 facilement. 3 finalement. 4 heureusement. 5 attentivement. 6 lentement. 7 complètement. 8 normalement. 9 principalement. 10 temporairement.

Exercise 27: 1 Le rapport? Il est très important. 2 La bière? Elle est mauvaise. 3 La poche? Elle est pleine. 4 L'appareil? Il est excellent. 5 Le restaurant? Il est fermé.

6 La qualité? Elle est très bonne. 7 Les produits? Ils sont
français. 8 Les messages? Ils sont en anglais.
9 L'explication? Elle n'est pas claire. 10 Le répondeur
automatique? Il n'est pas cher.

Exercise 28: 1 Oui, elle vous cherche. 2 Oui, elle me
consulte. 3 Oui, je le rencontre. 4 Oui, je la copie. 5 Oui, il
l'invite. 6 Oui, il les exporte. 7 Oui, nous le comprenons.
8 Oui, nous la branchons. 9 Oui, nous le mettons en
marche. 10 Oui, nous le copions. 11 Oui, elles nous
répondent en français. 12 Oui, ils lui téléphonent.
13 Oui, ils lui téléphonent. 14 Oui, ils leur téléphonent.
15 Oui, je lui parle. 16 Oui, je leur réponds. 17 Oui, je leur
défends de rentrer tard.

Exercise 29: 1 Oui, je l'ai invité. 2 Oui, je l'ai invitée.
3 Oui, je les ai invités. 4 Oui, il les a exportées. 5 Oui, elle l'a
consulté. 6 Oui, elle l'a consultée. 7 Oui, elle les a consultés.
8 Oui, ils l'ont branchée. 9 Oui, ils les ont réservées. 10 Oui,
ils l'ont perdue. 11 Oui, nous l'avons compris. 12 Oui, nous
l'avons comprise. 13 Oui, nous les avons comprises. 14 Oui,
nous les avons compris. 15 Oui, je l'ai mise dans ma poche.

CHAPTER 6

Exercise 30: 1 Il y a une serviette sur la table. 2 Il y a un taxi
devant l'hôtel. 3 Il y a un restaurant derrière l'église. 4 Il y a
un supermarché à côté de la banque. 5 Il y a une librairie en
face de l'université. 6 Est-ce qu'il y a une cabine télphonique
près de la gare? 7 Est-ce qu'il y a des livres américain à la
bibliothèque? 8 Est-ce qu'il y a un tunnel sous la Manche?
9 Je vais au cinéma. 10 Elle va aux États-Unis. 11 Avez-vous
le numéro de téléphone du théâtre? 12 J'ai acheté un journal
pour mon ami(e). 13 Elle apprend le français avec des cassettes. 14 C'est difficile de travailler sans ma secrétaire.
15 Mangeons après le spectacle. 16 Téléphonons avant 9
heures.

Exercise 31: 1 Le banquier est plus riche que le professeur.
2 Le facteur est plus pauvre que l'avocat. 3 L'hôtesse de l'air
est plus belle que l'actrice. 4 La lettre est moins importante
que le télégramme. 5 Le pilote est aussi courageux que l'astronaute. 6 Le français n'est pas si difficile que le russe.

7 Elle parle plus distinctement que Paul. 8 Il écoute plus attentivement que son frère.

Exercise 32: 1 Oui, c'est le restaurant le plus chic du monde. 2 Oui, c'est la plus grande librairie du monde. 3 Oui, c'est le magasin le plus célèbre du monde. 4 Oui, c'est la plus belle cathédrale du monde. 5 Oui, c'est la meilleure bière du monde. 6 Oui, c'est le parc le plus agréable du monde. 7 Oui, c'est la ville la plus intéressante du monde. 8 Oui, c'est la voiture la plus confortable du monde. 9 Oui, c'est l'avion le plus impressionnant du monde.

Exercise 33: 1 Il pleut. 2 Il fait du brouillard. 3 Il fait du vent. 4 Il fait froid. 5 Il fait du soleil. 6 Il neige. 7 Il fait chaud. 8 Il fait mauvais. 9 Il fait beau.

Exercise 34: A. 1 Je suis médecin. 2 Ce matin je suis arrivé à l'hôpital à 7 heures. 3 Je suis allé à une réunion à 10 heures. 4 Je suis parti avec deux infirmières. B. 1 Je suis journaliste. 2 Hier je suis allée à une conférence de presse. 3 Je suis montée au restaurant à une heure. 4 Je suis retournée au bureau très tard. C. 1 Nicole et Sophie sont étudiantes. 2 Ce matin elles sont allées à l'université à 9 heures. 3 Elles sont restées toute la journée à la bibliothèque. 4 Elles sont revenues à la maison à 5 heures.

Exercise 35: 1 Les ingénieurs sont arrivés hier. 2 Les actrices sont déjà parties. 3 Nous sommes revenues tôt. 4 Tu es descendu. 5 Est-ce que l'infirmière est restée toute la journée? 6 Etes-vous revenu très tard?

Exercise 36: 1 Je voudrais une carte postale. 2 Je voudrais un timbre. 3 Je voudrais un plan de la ville. 4 Je voudrais un journal américain. 5 Je voudrais du lait. 6 Je voudrais du sucre. 7 Je voudrais du thé. 8 Je voudrais téléphoner à New York. 9 Je voudrais envoyer un télégramme. 10 Je voudrais régler la note.

Exercise 37: 1 Il me faut un crayon. 2 Il me faut un stylo-bille. 3 Il lui faut une gomme. 4 Il lui faut du papier à lettres. 5 Il leur faut des enveloppes. 6 Il leur faut des cigarettes. 7 Il leur faut des allumettes.

CHAPTER 7

Exercise 38: 1 Non, j'ai beaucoup de cravates. 2 Non, j'ai
beaucoup de mouchoirs. 3 Non, j'ai beaucoup de robes.
4 Oui, il a maintenant trop de pantalons. 5 Oui, elle a maintenant trop de jupes. 6 Oui, elle a maintenant trop de foulards.
7 Il a peu de patience. 8 Avez-vous (or as-tu) mis assez de
chemises de nuit dans la valise? 9 J'ai plus de cardigans que
Monique. 10 Vous avez moins de costumes que Pierre.

Exercise 39: 1 Je vais écouter la radio. 2 Je vais acheter un
journal. 3 Je vais étudier le français. 4 Je vais faire mes
courses. 5 Il réparera la voiture. 6 Il jouera au tennis.
7 Il écrira une lettre. 8 Il visitera le musée. 9 Ils tapisseront
l'appartement. 10 Ils organiseront une réunion. 11 Ils iront à
une conférence internationale. 12 Ils passeront un week-end
à Londres. 13 Elle finira sa lettre. 14 Nous irons au théâtre la
semaine prochaine. 15 Vous surprendrez votre père.
16 Tu choisiras ta robe le mois prochain.

Exercise 40: 1 Je peux acheter les légumes au marché.
2 Je peux préparer le rapport. 3 Nous ne pouvons pas arriver
lundi. 4 Nous ne pouvons pas lire son écriture. 5 Elle doit
signer le contrat. 6 Elle doit arrêter de fumer. 7 Ils ne
doivent pas décourager les étudiants. 8 Ils ne doivent pas
garer la voiture devant l'hôpital. 9 Il veut faire le tour du
monde. 10 Il veut dépenser moins d'argent. 11 Savez-vous
(or sais-tu) conduire? 12 Savez-vous (or sais-tu) nager?

Exercise 41: Examples: 1 L'Allemagne (f.). 2 L'Autriche (f.).
3 La Belgique. 4 Le Danemark. 5 L'Espagne (f.).
6 La Finlande. 7 La France. 8 La Grèce. 9 La Hollande.
10 L'Italie (f.) 11 Le Luxembourg. 12 Le Portugal. 13 La
République d'Irlande. 14 Le Royaume-Uni. 15 La Suède.

Exercise 42: 1 Nous passons nos vacances en Grèce.
2 Avez-vous l'intention d'aller au Japon?
3 La Grande-Bretagne exporte des voitures en France.
4 Est-ce que le diplomate est arrivé en Russie?

Exercise 43: a) Vingt. b) Vingt-deux. c) Trente et un.
d) Quarante-sept. e) Cinquante-neuf. f) Soixante et un.
g) Soixante-dix. h) Soixante-dix-neuf. i) Quatre-vingt-un.
j) Quatre-vingt-onze. k) Quatre-vingt-dix-neuf. l) Cent.

CHAPTER 8

Exercise 44: 1 Il jouait au football. 2 Il allait à la pêche.
3 Il collectionnait des timbres. 4 Elle chantait. 5 Elle écoutait
des disques. 6 Nous apprenions l'espagnol. 7 Nous habitions
dans une petite maison. 8 Nous faisions de la photo(graphie).
9 Je finissais la traduction quand j'ai entendu un bruit en
haut. 10 Elle faisait les courses quand elle a perdu son porte-
monnaie. 11 Ils regardaient la télévision quand le
cambrioleur est entré dans la maison.

Exercise 45: 1 L'hôtel, que vous cherchez, est à droite.
2 Je voudrais la chambre qui donne sur le parc. 3 La chambre,
que nous avons réservée pour vous, est à côté de l'ascenseur.
4 J'ai apporté le petit déjeuner que votre mari a commandé.
5 Où est le poste de télévision qui ne marche pas?
6 Les valises, qui sont dans le vestibule, sont très lourdes.
7 La réceptionniste, à qui vous avez parlé, est bilingue.
8 Le client, dont le fils est malade, est dans la chambre 5.
9 N'avez-vous pas compris ce que la femme de chambre
vous a dit? 10 La note, que vous avez préparée, est correcte.

Exercise 46: 1 Si j'étais riche, je ferais le tour du monde.
2 Si je ne travaillais pas, je peindrais et je dessinerais.
3 S'il avait beaucoup de temps, il apprendrait le portugais.
4 Si elle parlait français, elle travaillerait comme interprète.
5 Si elle parlait allemand, elle travaillerait comme secrétaire
bilingue. 6 Si vous étiez marié, vous rentreriez plus tôt le
soir à la maison. 7 S'ils étaient en chômage, ils chercheraient
du travail. 8 Si elles avaient des enfants, elles resteraient à la
maison. 9 Si j'avais le temps, je lirais beaucoup. 10 Si nous
voulions maigrir, nous mangerions moins et ferions de la
gymnastique.

Exercise 47: 1 … avec lui. 2 … à côté d'elle. 3 … sans
 eux. 4 … qu'elles. 5 … que lui. 6 … Elle. 7 Ce sont (or
C'est) eux qui …

Exercise 48: 1 Je ne sais pas si Paul a fini son travail.
2 Je ne connais pas les Dupont. 3 Savez-vous où je peux
louer une machine à écrire? 4 Savez-vous si le médecin est
libre? 5 Est-ce que Marie-Claude connaît ma tante?

Exercise 49: Je ne vous dérange pas. Je pensais justement à vous. Vous n'êtes pas trop occupée? ... quand vous avez frappé à la porte. À qui est-ce que vous écriviez? À propos, comment va votre travail? Qu'est-ce que vous feriez de tout ce temps libre? Vous feriez mieux de prendre votre retraite. tout de suite

SELF-ASSESSMENT TEST 2

A: 1 devant. 2 à côté de. 3 en face de. 4 sous. 5 près de. 6 sans. 7 après. 8 avant.

B: 1 Je suis journaliste. 2 Ce matin, je suis arrivé(e) à l'hôtel à sept heures. 3 Je suis allé(e) à une conférence internationale à dix heures. 4 Je suis parti(e) très tard.

C: 1 Il pleut. 2 Il fait chaud. / Il fait du soleil. 3 Il fait/Il y a du brouillard. 4 Il fait froid. / Il neige. 5 Il fait froid. / Il fait du vent.

D: 1 le Portugal. 2 le Japon. 3 les États-Unis. 4 la Grèce. 5 l'Espagne. 6 l'Italie. 7 la Hollande / les Pays-Bas. 8 la Chine. 9 la Belgique. 10 la France. 11 l'Angleterre. 12 le Danemark.

E: a) cinquante-huit. b) soixante-dix. c) soixante-quinze. d) quatre-vingt-trois. e) quatre-vingt-dix. f) quatre-vingt-dix-neuf. g) cent.

F: 1 Il jouait au football. 2 Elle apprenait l'anglais. 3 Ils habitaient dans une grande maison. 4 Ils faisaient les courses quand elle a perdu son porte-monnaie.

G: 1 Si j'étais riche, je visiterais le Japon et la Chine. 2 Si elle parlait italien, elle travaillerait comme secrétaire bilingue. 3 Si tu étais au chômage, tu chercherais du travail. 4 Si nous avions beaucoup de temps, nous lirions beaucoup.

H: a) Savoir means "to know a fact." Connaître is used with the meaning of "to be acquainted with" (people, places, etc.). b) Je ne sais pas jouer ... means "I do not know how to ...;" je ne peux pas jouer ... means something (such as a broken finger) prevents me from playing.

I: • J'ai décidé de changer ma vie. Je vais regarder la télévision moins souvent. Je mangerai plus de fruits. Je ferai de la gymnastique chaque matin. Je dépenserai moins d'argent en vêtements. • Oui, j'aurai plus de temps et plus d'argent, et je serai en meilleure santé.

Score 80%-100% = excellent. You've done really well! 60% – 79% = very good. 45%-59% = satisfactory – try to find time to study a little every day. Below 45% = you must review. It's important to consolidate your knowledge before going on.

CHAPTER 9

Exercise 50: 1 Mon rhume est pire que celui de ma soeur. 2 Cet hôpital est plus moderne que celui que la Princesse a visité l'année dernière. 3 Quel chirurgien a effectué la greffe du coeur? Celui-ci ou celui-là? 4 Avez-vous rendez-vous (or un rendez-vous) avec ce dentiste-ci ou celui-là? 5 Le (la) kinésithérapeute m'a donné ceci. 6 Le pharmacien a préparé cela. 7 C'est votre nouvelle secrétaire. 8 Ce sont vos malades.

Exercise 51: 1 Le barman vous a servi votre whisky, mais où est le mien? 2 Mon poisson est délicieux; le vôtre n'est pas frais. 3 J'ai payé notre addition et ils ont payé la leur. 4 Est-ce que ce chapeau est à vous ou à votre ami? 5 Avec quoi voulez-vous manger ce repas chinois? Avec des baguettes? Quoi? Non! Avec un couteau et une fourchette. 6 Quel est le numéro de téléphone du restaurant italien? 7 Quels légumes a-t-elle commandés? 8 Qu'est-ce qui sent si bon? 9 Voici une liste des meilleurs restaurants de Paris; lequel préférez-vous? 10 A qui est cette cuillère?

Exercise 52: 1 Elle tape lentement à la machine. 2 Ils chantent mal. 3 Ne parlez pas si bas. 4 Il va souvent chez ses parents. 5 Nous avons déjà mangé. 6 Il va sûrement pleuvoir ou neiger. 7 Elle prend un bain en bas. 8 Elles ont fait les courses hier.

CHAPTER 10

Exercise 53: 1 Il se réveille à 7 heures du matin. 2 Il se lave. 3 Il se rase. 4 Il va au travail. 5 Elle se lève à 8 heures du matin. 6 Elle prend une douche. 7 Elle se peigne. 8 Elle se maquille. 9 Elle va à la gare. 10 Nous nous lavons. 11 Nous

nous habillons vite. 12 Nous nous promenons. 13 Nous
nous couchons à dix heures du soir. 14 Je me suis amusée.
15 Vous ne vous êtes pas trompée. 16 Elles se reposent. 17
Ils ont lavé la voiture eux-mêmes. 18 Nous nous brossons les
dents chaque matin.

Exercise 54: 1 Il a quitté la maison sans dire un mot. 2 Elle
est habituée à écouter des disques dans sa chambre. 3 Avant
de réparer la lampe, il a téléphoné à l'électricien. 4 Après
avoir préparé le petit déjeuner, elle a fait le ménage.
5 Ma mère a commencé par dire que toute la famille était en
bonne santé et a fini par souhaiter à tout le monde une
bonne année. 6 Ce poste de radio est excellent pour capter
les émissions françaises.

Exercise 55: 1 J'ai l'intention d'acheter des lunettes de soleil.
2 Sera-t-il possible de faire des excursions? 3 Nous préférons
louer un appartement. 4 Ils m'ont invitée à aller à la pêche.
5 J'hésite à faire du ski nautique. 6 Aurez-vous l'occasion de
faire de la planche à voile?

Exercise 56: 1 Est-ce-que vous me l'avez donné? 2 Il nous
les a promises. 3 Il a l'intention de me les vendre. 4 Je le lui
ai envoyé. 5 Il la lui montre. 6 Nous les leur avons données.

CHAPTER 11

Exercise 57: 1 Comme (or puisque) l'ami de Paul vient
camper avec nous, nous devrons acheter un lit de camp
supplémentaire. 2 Quand vous saurez parler français, nous
irons faire du camping en France. 3 Saisissez-vous chaque
occasion pour parler français, quand vous êtes en Belgique?
4 Je n'aime pas ce camping parce qu'il n'y a pas de piscine.
5 Nous sommes quatre mais nous avons seulement (or nous
n'avons que) trois sacs de couchage. 6 La voiture est tombée
en panne, donc nous avons décidé de camper dans un champ.

Exercise 58: a) deux cent cinquante. b) trois cents. c) quatre
cent trente. d) cinq cent soixante-dix. e) six cent quatre-
vingts. f) mille quatre cent quarante.

Exercise 59: 1 la première discothèque. 2 le deuxième
(second) casino. 3 la troisième boîte de nuit 4 le quatrième

théâtre. 5 le cinquième concert. 6 le sixième opéra.
7 le septième cinéma. 8 la huitième patinoire. 9 le neuvième
ballet. 10 le dixième restaurant.

Exercise 60: 1 L'importance de la décision a été soulignée par
le président de la République française. 2 La Grande-Bretagne
sera reliée au continent par un tunnel ferroviaire en 1993.
3 Un lien routier sera construit plus tard. 4 Cette décision
historique a été annoncée à Lille. 5 Les touristes étrangers ont
souvent été découragés par la traversée de la Manche.

Exercise 61: 1 Elle s'est cassé le bras en faisant du ski.
2 Je suis tombé en patinant. 3 En allant aux cours du soir
trois fois par semaine, il a obtenu son diplôme. 4 Voyant
que l'automobiliste était blessé, l'agent de police a appelé
une ambulance. 5 En téléphonant.vous aurez la réponse
tout de suite.

Exercise 62: 1 Téléphonez-lui – non, ne lui téléphonez pas.
2 Envoyez-leur cette brochure – non, ne la leur envoyez pas.
3 Copiez ce document – non, ne le copiez pas. 4 Donnez-moi
le catalogue – non, ne me le donnez pas. 5 Envoyez-lui les
échantillons – non, ne les lui envoyez pas. 6 Tapez cette
lettre – non, ne la tapez pas. 7 Soyez ici à 9 heures – non, à 8
heures. 8 Voulez-vous bien faire des heures supplémentaires?

Exercise 63: 1 Je suis marié depuis cinq ans. 2 J'habite dans
cette maison depuis quatre ans. 3 Je travaille pour cette
banque depuis trois ans. 4 J'ai cette voiture depuis deux ans.
5 J'apprends à jouer du piano depuis un an.

Exercise 64: 1 Mais je viens d'appeler un docteur. 2 Mais je
viens de prévenir les pompiers. 3 Mais je viens de vous
montrer mon permis de conduire. 4 Mais les ambulanciers
viennent de transporter les blessés à l'hôpital. 5 Mais je
viens de vous donner mon adresse.

CHAPTER 12

Exercise 65: 1 Qu'est-ce que vous faites dans la vie?
2 Ma soeur fait une tarte aux pommes. 3 Je vais faire une
conférence sur la psychologie devant 200 personnes.

4 Elle a fait une promenade au parc hier. 5 Il fait de la fièvre.
6 Ne fais pas l'idiot. 7 J'ai fait travailler mon fils. 8 Je me fais
construire une maison à Avignon.

Exercise 66: 1 he gave. 2 I sold. 3 we finished. 4 she had.
5 I was. 6 you had. 7 he took. 8 she went out. 9 they read.
10 they put.

Exercise 67: 1 Je suggère que le président fasse une déclaration
à la télévision. 2 Il faut que nous continuions notre conquête
de l'espace. 3 Il voudrait que le lancement du vaisseau spatial
ait lieu la semaine prochaine. 4 Je suis content que vous
participiez à cette mission spatiale. 5 Il est important que le
lancement soit filmé en direct. 6 A moins que vous ne
puissiez me donner toutes les données enregistrées par les
ordinateurs, je ne peux pas prendre de décision. 7 Nous
sommes contents que le président ait décidé de reporter son
discours. 8 Bien que les astronautes soient habitués à
l'apesanteur, ils ont quand même un peu de mal à mener
leurs expériences à bord du vaisseau spatial.

SELF-ASSESSMENT TEST 3

A: 1 Je me réveille à huit heures du matin. 2 Je me lave.
3 Je me rase. 4 Je vais au travail. 5 Monique se lève à neuf
heures. 6 Elle se lave. 7 Elle s'habille vite. 8 Elle va au
bureau. 9 (Hier) Nicole et moi, nous nous sommes réveillées
à dix heures. 10 Nous nous sommes maquillées.
11 Nous sommes allées à la gare.

B: 1 sans dire. 2 avant de répondre. 3 par critiquer.
4 Après avoir acheté.

C: 1 car/parce que. 2 donc. 3 Pendant que. 4 mais.
5 Quand/Aussitôt que.

D: a) quatre cent quarante. b) trois cents. c) sept cent quatre-
vingts. d) trois cent dix. e) mille trois cent trente. f) cinq cents.

E: 1 Depuis quand es-tu en États-Unis?/Depuis combien de
temps es-tu en États-Unis? 2 Je travaille ici depuis le deux
mai. 3 Nous apprenons le français depuis trois mois.
4 Nous venons d'acheter un appartement. 5 Ils viennent
d'appeler un médecin/docteur.

F: 1 Nous espérons aller à la plage. 2 Ils ont décidé de louer une voiture. 3 Elles sont contentes de voir le soleil. 4 Elle a l'intention d'acheter des lunetttes de soleil. 5 J'hésite à faire du ski nautique. 6 Auras-tu l'occasion de faire de la planche à voile?

G: 1 Qu'est-ce que vous faites dans la vie? 2 Ma mère fait un gâteau. 3 Je vais faire une conférence sur la conquête de l'espace devant cent personnes. 4 Il a fait une promenade au parc.

H: 1 Copiez-la – non, ne la copiez pas. 2 Envoyez-les – non, ne les envoyez pas. 3 Donnez-le-moi – non, ne me le donnez pas. 4 Téléphonez-leur – non, ne leur téléphonez pas.

I: 1 Je voudrais que vous fixiez un rendez-vous. 2 Je veux bien vous aider, à condition que vous finissiez le travail aujourd'hui. 3 Il est dommage que Sophie ne vienne pas à la réception. 4 Nous sommes contents qu'ils aient trouvé une petite maison.

J: • Oui, bien sûr. Je les ai achetées parce que je dois apprendre l'anglais en trois mois. • Oui, je les écoute le matin quand je me lave. Mon mari les écoute aussi, quand il se rase. Si je réussis à apprendre l'anglais, il me sera possible d'obtenir une promotion et de voyager aux États-Unis.

Score: 80%-100% = congratulations – you've made full use of this course! 60%-79% = well done! With a little review you'll be able to improve your score. 45%-59% = satisfactory. Remember that the key to greater success is daily study and repetition. Below 45% = much more review needed. Try writing out all the new words and expressions, since this helps you remember them.

Mini-dictionary

This mini-dictionary contains the most important words found in the book plus others that you may find useful. Numbers at the end of some entries indicate chapters and sections where irregular verbs and other important points are explained. See sections 23–26 for seasons, months of the year, dates, and days of the week.

English – French

able, to be able pouvoir *sec. 48*
above au-dessus de
abroad à l'étranger
actress actrice
address adresse *(f.)*
advance, in advance à l'avance
advertisement annonce *(f.)*
advertising publicité *(f.)*
advise conseiller
after après
afternoon après-midi *(m or f)*
afterwards ensuite
again encore
agency agence *(f.)*
ago il y a
agree: I agree je suis d'accord
Aids sida *(m.)*
air-conditioning climatisation *(f.)*
airline company compagnie *(f.)* aérienne
alcohol alcool *(m.)*
all tout *page 94*
allow permettre *(irreg.) sec. 30*
already déjà
also aussi

although bien que, quoique
always toujours
ambulance ambulance *(f.)*
ambulance driver ambulancier *(m.)*, -ière *(f.)*
America Amérique *(f.)*
American américain, Américain *(m.)*, -e *(f.)*
analyze analyser
and et
announce annoncer *sec. 81*
answer *(vb.)* répondre
antique dealer antiquaire *(m. & f.)*
apartment appartement *(m.)*
apple pomme *(f.)*
appointment rendez-vous *(m.)*
appreciate apprécier
approve (of) approuver
arm bras *(m.)*
armchair fauteuil *(m.)*
arrive arriver
ask (for) demander
astronaut astronaute *(m & f.)*
attach attacher

234

aunt tante
auto-body shop garage *(m.)*
avoid éviter

bad mauvais
badly mal
bag sac *(m.)*
bakery boulangerie *(f.)*
ballpoint pen stylo-bille *(m.)*
bank banque *(f.)*
banker banquier *(m.)*
bar bar *(m.)*
bath bain *(m.)*
be, to be être *(irreg.) sec. 6*
beach plage *(f.)*
beautiful beau *chapter 6*
because parce que
bed lit *(m.)*
   to go to bed se coucher
bedroom chambre *(f.)*
beer bière *(f.)*
before avant
begin commencer *sec. 81*
behind derrière
Belgium Belgique *(f.)*
better meilleur, mieux
between entre
bicycle bicyclette *(f.)*, vélo *(m.)*
big grand
bilingual bilingue
bill addition, note *(f.)*
blood pressure tension *(f.)*
blue bleu
boat bateau *(m.)*
book livre *(m.)*
book *(vb.)* réserver
bookstore librairie *(f.)*
boring ennuyeux
   to be bored s'ennuyer *sec. 81*
boss patron *(m.)*,-onne *(f.)*
bottle bouteille *(f.)*
brand marque *(f.)*
brave courageux
bread pain *(m.)*
break *(vb.)* casser
breakdown panne *(f.)*

break down tomber en panne
breakfast petit déjeuner *(m.)*
briefcase serviette *(f.)*
bring apporter, amener *sec. 81*
bring down descendre
bring up monter
Britain Grande-Bretagne *(f.)*
British britannique
broadcast émission *(f.)*
brochure brochure *(f.)*
brother frère
brown brun
build construire *(irreg.) page 176*
burglar cambrioleur *(m.)*
burn *(vb.)* brûler
bus autobus *(m.)*
business affaires *(f. pl.)*
businessman homme d'affaires
busy occupé
but mais
butcher's boucherie *(f.)*
buy acheter *sec. 81*

cake gâteau *(m.)*
call *(vb.)* appeler, *sec. 81*
   to be called s'appeler
camera appareil-photo *(m.)*
camp *(vb.)* camper
can (to be able) pouvoir *(irreg.)*
   sec. 48
Canada Canada *(m.)*
cancel annuler
car voiture *(f.)*
card carte *(f.)*
cash: to pay in cash payer en
   espèces
cash register caisse *(f.)*
castle château *(m.)*
cathedral cathédrale *(f.)*
chambermaid femme de
   chambre
change *(vb.)* changer *sec. 81*
Channel Manche *(f.)*
check chèque *(m.)*
check *(vb.)* vérifier
cheese fromage *(m.)*

China Chine *(f.)*
Chinese chinois, Chinois *(m.)*
 –e *(f.)*
choose choisir
church église *(f.)*
clean *(vb.)* nettoyer *sec. 81*
client client *(m.)*, -e *(f.)*
close *(vb.)* fermer
clothes vêtements *(m. pl.)*
coach car *(m.)*
coffee café *(m.)*
cold froid
 to be cold avoir froid
 to have a cold avoir un rhume
color couleur *(f.)*
come venir *(irreg.)* pages 93/94
comfortable confortable
complaint plainte *(f.)*
computer ordinateur *(m.)*
 (computer) software logiciel
 (m.)
conference conférence *(f.)*
confirm confirmer
congratulate féliciter
consult consulter
continue continuer
contract contrat *(m.)*
copy *(vb.)* copier
correct *(vb.)* corriger *sec. 81*
cost *(vb.)* coûter
country pays *(m.)*
create créer
credit card carte *(f.)* de crédit
criticize critiquer
cross *(vb.)* traverser
cup tasse *(f.)*
customs douane *(f.)*
cut *(vb.)* couper

dance *(vb.)* danser
dangerous dangereux
date date *(f.)*; rendez-vous *(m.)*
daughter fille
dear cher
decide décider
deep profond

degree (univ.) licence *(f.)*
delicious délicieux
dentist dentiste *(m. & f.)*
departure départ *(m.)*
deposit: to leave a deposit
 verser des arrhes *(f. pl.)*
dial *(vb.)* composer (un numéro)
dictionary dictionnaire *(m.)*
diet régime *(m.)*
difficult difficile
dinner dîner *(m.)*
director directeur *(m.)*, -trice *(f.)*
dirty sale
disco discothèque *(f.)*
discourage décourager *sec. 81*
discuss discuter de
disease maladie *(f.)*
 "mad cow" disease maladie de
 la "vache folle"
disembark débarquer
dish plat *(m.)*
disturb déranger *sec. 81*
dive *(vb.)* plonger
do faire *(irreg.) sec. 77*
doctor médecin, docteur *(m.)*
doubt *(vb.)* douter
downstairs en bas
dress robe *(f.)*
drink *(vb.)* boire *(irreg.)* page 117
drive *(vb.)* conduire *(irreg.) page
 113* rouler
driver's license permis *(m.)* de
 conduire
drugstore pharmacie

each chaque
early tôt
earn gagner
east est *(m.)*
easy facile
eat manger *sec. 81*
efficient efficace
electrician électricien *(m.)*
elevator ascenseur *(m.)*
embassy ambassade *(f.)*

236

emergency: in an emergency en
cas d'urgence
encourage encourager *sec. 81*
end fin *(f.)*
engine moteur *(m.)*
engineer ingénieur *(m.)*
England Angleterre *(f.)*
English anglais
enjoy oneself s'amuser
enough assez
enter entrer
entertainment distractions *(f. pl.)*
envelope enveloppe *(f.)*
especially surtout
European Union Union
européenne
even même
evening soir *(m.)*
everyone tout le monde
everything tout
everywhere partout
exactly exactement
excellent excellent
excursion excursion *(f.)*
expensive cher
explanation explication *(f.)*
export exporter
extra supplément *(m.)*

fall *(vb.)* tomber
family famille *(f.)*
famous célèbre
far loin
fashion mode *(f.)*
fast rapide
father père
fever fièvre *(f.)*
field champ *(m.)*
fill remplir
film film *(m.)*
    (for snapshots) pellicule *(f.)*
find trouver
fine beau; bien
finish *(vb.)* finir
fire incendie *(m.)*
fire exit sortie *(f.)* de secours

fire fighter pompier
first premier
fish poisson *(m.)*
fishing pêche *(f.)*
    to go fishing aller à la pêche
fish market poissonnerie *(f.)*
flag drapeau *(m.)*
flight vol *(m.)*
fog brouillard *(m.)*
food nourriture *(f.)*
for pour
forbid défendre
foreign étranger
forget oublier
forgive pardonner
fork fourchette *(f.)*
fortunately heureusement
free libre
French français
fresh frais, fraîche *(f.)*
friend ami *(m.)*, -e *(f.)*
from de
front: in front of devant
fruit fruit(s) *(m.)*
full plein

gasoline essence *(f.)*
generally généralement
German allemand
Germany Allemagne *(f.)*
get obtenir *(irreg.) page 167*
get up se lever *sec. 81*
gift cadeau *(m.)*
give donner
give back rendre
glad content
glass verre *(m.)*
glove gant *(m.)*
go aller *(irreg.) pages 93/94*
go down descendre
go out sortir *(irreg.) page 167*
go up monter
good bon, bonne *(f.)*
good-bye au revoir
government gouvernement *(m.)*
gray gris

Great Britain Grande-Bretagne *(f.)*
Greece Grèce *(f.)*
grocer's épicerie *(f.)*
group groupe *(m.)*
guarantee *(vb.)* garantir
guide guide *(m.)*
guidebook guide *(m.)*

haggle marchander
hair cheveux *(m. pl.)*
hairdresser coiffeur *(m.)*, -euse
    (f.)
half moitié *(f.)*
hall vestibule *(m.)*
ham jambon *(m.)*
hand main *(f.)*
handkerchief mouchoir *(m.)*
handwriting écriture *(f.)*
happen arriver, se passer
happy heureux
harbor port *(m.)*
hat chapeau *(m.)*
hate *(vb.)* détester
have avoir *(irreg.) sec.* 4
have to (must) devoir *(irreg.) sec.*
    48
hay fever rhume *(m.)* des foins
head tête *(f.)*
health santé *(f.)*
hear entendre
heart coeur *(m.)*
heavy lourd
help *(vb.)* aider
her *sec. 19, 33, 54*
hers *sec. 57*
here ici
here is voici
highway autoroute *(f.)*
his *sec. 19, 57*
hope *(vb.)* espérer *sec. 81*
horrible affreux
hospital hôpital *(m.)*
hot chaud
hotel hôtel *(m.)*
house maison *(f.)*
hovercraft aéroglisseur *(m.)*

how comment
how much, how many combien
hungry: to be hungry avoir faim
hurry se dépêcher
husband mari

ice glace *(f.)*
ice cream glace *(f.)*
identification pièce *(f.)* d'identité
ill malade
immediately tout de suite
import importer
important important
impossible impossible
impressive impressionnant
improve améliorer
included compris
income revenu *(m.)*
increase *(vb.)* augmenter
increase augmentation *(f.)*
inexpensive pas cher
information renseignement(s)
    (m.)
injured blessé
interesting intéressant
interpreter interprète *(m. & f.)*
invite inviter
invoice facture *(f.)*
Ireland Irlande *(f.)*
Irish irlandais

jacket veste *(f.)*
jam confiture *(f.)*
Japan Japon *(m.)*
Japanese japonais
job emploi *(m.)*, poste *(m.)*
journalist journaliste *(m. & f.)*

keep *(vb.)* garder
key clé *(f.)*
kind aimable
kitchen cuisine *(f.)*
knife couteau *(m.)*
knock *(vb.)* frapper
know savoir *(irreg.) sec. 48,*
    connaître *(irreg.) sec. 55*

lady dame
lake lac *(m.)*
lamp lampe *(f.)*
land terre *(f.)*
language langue *(f.)*
large grand
last dernier
late en retard
law loi *(f.)*
lawyer avocat *(m.)*, -e *(f.)*
learn apprendre *(irreg.) sec. 29*
leather cuir *(m.)*
leave *(vb.)* partir *(irreg.) page 55,*
    quitter
lecture conférence *(f.)*
left: on/to the left à gauche
leg jambe *(f.)*
less moins
lesson leçon *(f.)*
letter lettre *(f.)*
library bibliothèque *(f.)*
life vie *(f.)*
like *(vb.)* aimer
line up *(vb.)* faire la queue
listen (to) écouter
live habiter, vivre *(irreg.)*
    page 185
long long, longue *(f.)*
look (at) regarder
look for chercher
lose perdre
loud fort
lounge chair chaise *(f.)* lounge
luck chance *(f.)*
luggage bagages *(m. usu.pl.)*
lunch déjeuner *(m.)*

machine appareil *(m.)*, machine
    (f.)
magazine revue *(f.)*
mail courrier *(m.)*
mailman facteur
main principal
make faire *(irreg.) sec. 77*
managing director (and
    chairman) président-directeur
    général *(m.)*

many beaucoup (de)
map carte *(f.)*, plan *(m.)*
market marché *(m.)*
marriage mariage *(m.)*
married marié
    to get married se marier
match allumette *(f.)*
match (sports) match *(m.)*
match (light) allumette *(f.)*
me me, moi
meal repas *(m.)*
meat viande *(f.)*
mechanic mécanicien *(m.)*
medicine médicament *(m.)*
meet rencontrer
meeting réunion *(f.)*
message message *(m.)*
method méthode *(f.)*
midday midi *(m.)*
midnight minuit *(m.)*
milk lait *(m.)*
mine mien *(m.)*, -ne *(f.) sec. 57*
mistake erreur *(f.)*
    to make a mistake se tromper
modern moderne
moment instant, moment *(m.)*
money argent *(m.)*
month mois *(m.)*
mood humeur *(f.)*
more plus
morning matin *(m.)*
mother mère
motorbike moto *(f.)*
motorist automobiliste *(m. & f.)*
mountain montagne *(f.)*
much beaucoup (de)
    as much/many autant (de)
    so much/many tant (de)
museum musée *(m.)*
music musique *(f.)*
must (to have to) devoir *(irreg.)*
    sec. 48
my mon, ma, mes

name nom *(m.)*
napkin serviette *(f.)*
near près *(adv.)* près de *(prep.)*

necessary nécessaire
need *sec. 45*
neighbor voisin *(m.)* -e *(f.)*
nephew neveu
never jamais, ne [verb] jamais
new neuf, neuve *(f.)*, nouveau
  sec. 27
news nouvelle(s) *(f.)*
newspaper journal *(m.)*
next prochain
next to à côté de
night nuit *(f.)*
nightclub boîte *(f.)* de nuit
nightgown chemise *(f.)* de nuit
noise bruit *(m.)*
noisy, bruyant
no non
no longer ne [verb] plus
no one personne, ne [verb]
  personne
normal normal
north nord *(m.)*
nose nez *(m.)*
note (message) petie mot *(m.)*
nothing rien, ne [verb] rien
now maintenant
nuisance: that's a nuisance c'est
  énervant
number numéro *(m.)*
nurse infirmier *(m.)*, -ière *(f.)*

obey obéir
obtain obtenir *(irreg.) page 167*
obvious évident
occasionally de temps en temps
occupied occupé
of de
odd bizarre
offend offenser
offer offre *(f.)*
office bureau
often souvent
oil huile *(f.)*
old vieux, vieille *(f.) sec. 27*
on sur
only seul, seulement

open *(vb.)* ouvrir *(irreg.)* j'ouvre,
  nous ouvrons; j'ai ouvert
open ouvert
opera opéra *(m.)*
opinion avis *(m.)*
  in my opinion à mon avis
opportunity occasion *(f.)*
opposite en face *(adv.)*, en face de
  (prep.)
or ou
order *(vb.)* commander
  in order to pour, afin de
ordinary ordinaire
organize organiser
other autre
our notre, nos
ours le/la nôtre, les nôtres
overlook donner sur
overtime heures *(f.)*
  supplémentaires

pack *(vb.)* **(luggage)** faire ses
  valises *(f. pl.)*
pain douleur *(f.)*
paint *(vb.)* peindre *(irreg.) page
  128*
park parc *(m.)*
passport passeport *(m.)*
patient malade *(m. & f.)*
pay (for) payer *sec. 81*
pen stylo *(m.)*
pen (ballpoint) stylo *(m.)*
  bille
pencil crayon *(m.)*
people gens *(m. pl.)*
perfect *(vb.)* perfectionner
perfume parfum *(m.)*
perhaps peut-être
permit *(vb.)* permettre *(irreg.)*
  sec. 30
persuade persuader
photograph photo *(f.)*
photograph *(vb.)* prendre en
  photo
pick up (broadcast) capter

pity dommage (m.)
  what a pity! quel dommage!
plan projet (m.)
plane avion (m.)
play (vb.) jouer
pleasant agréable
please s'il vous plaît
please (vb.) plaire (irreg.) page 150
pleased content
pleasure plaisir (m.)
pocket poche (f.)
pocketbook sac à main
police officer agent de police
polite poli
poor pauvre
possible possible
postcard carte (f.) postale
post office bureau (m.) de poste
postpone reporter
practice pratiquer
prefer préférer sec. 81
prepare préparer
prescription ordonnance (f.)
press presse (f.)
press conference conférence (f.)
  de presse
pretty joli
prevent empêcher
price prix (m.)
probable probable
product produit (m.)
profession profession (f.)
promise (vb.) promettre (irreg.)
  sec. 30
psychology psychologie (f.)
purse porte-monnaie (m.)
put mettre (irreg.) sec. 30

qualifications diplômes (m. pl.)
quality qualité (f.)
quarrel dispute (f.)
quarrel (vb.) se disputer
queen reine
question question (f.)
  to ask a question poser une
  question

quick rapide
quickly vite, rapidement
quiet calme

rabies rage (f.)
radio radio (f.)
rain (vb.) pleuvoir (irreg.)
  it is raining il pleut
  it rained il a plu
rapid rapide
rash (skin) éruption (f.)
razor rasoir (m.)
read lire (irreg.) page 80
ready prêt
realize se rendre compte de
reason raison (f.)
reasonable raisonnable
receive recevoir (irreg.)
  je reçois, il reçoit, n. recevons,
  ils reçoivent;
  j'ai reçu, je recevrai
recently récemment
recommend recommander
record disque (m.)
record player électrophone (m.)
refuse (vb.) refuser
regret (vb.) regretter
remember se souvenir de (irreg.,
  conj. like venir) page 86
rent louer
repair (vb.) réparer
repeat répéter sec. 81
reply (vb.) répondre
reserve réserver
rest (vb.) se reposer
restaurant restaurant (m.)
return (vb.) retourner, rentrer
rich riche
right correct
  on/to the right à droite
  to be right avoir raison
room salle (f.)
  bedroom chambre (f.)
Russia Russie (f.)
Russian russe

sad triste
safe (valuables) coffre-fort (m.)
sailing: to go sailing faire de la
  voile
salad salade (f.)
salary salaire (m.)
sale vente (f.)
sales (bargains) soldes (m. pl.)
sand sable (m.)
say dire (irreg.) page 117
Scotland Écosse (f.)
Scottish écossais
sea mer (f.)
seat place (f.)
secretary secrétaire (m. & f.)
see voir (irreg.) less 11
sell vendre
send envoyer (irreg.) page 97
serious grave
serve servir (irreg.) page 145
settle régler sec. 81
several plusieurs
shave (vb.) raser, se raser
shirt chemise (f.)
shop magasin (m.)
shopping courses (f. pl.)
short court
show spectacle (m.)
show (vb.) montrer
shut (vb.) fermer
sign (vb.) signer
since depuis; puisque
sing chanter
single (ticket) aller (m.) simple
  (room) chambre (f.)
    individuelle
  (unmarried) célibataire
single European currency
  monnaie (f.) unique
    européenne
sister soeur
sit down s'asseoir (irreg.) page 167
size taille (f.)
skate (vb.) patiner
skating rink patinoire (f.)

ski (vb.) faire du ski
  waterskiing ski (m.) nautique
skirt jupe (f.)
sleep (vb.) dormir (irreg.)
  je dors, il dort, n. dormons;
  j'ai dormi
sleeping bag sac (m.) de
  couchage
slowly lentement
small petit
smell (vb.) sentir (irreg.)
  page 145
smoke (vb.) fumer
snow (vb.) neiger sec. 81
so si; donc
some sec. 1
something quelque chose
son fils
soon bientôt
  as soon as aussitôt que
sorry désolé
soup soupe (f.)
south sud (m.)
Spain Espagne (f.)
Spanish espagnol
speak parler
special offer promotion (f.)
spend (money) dépenser
spend (time) passer
spoon cuillère (f.)
sport sport (m.)
square place (f.)
stamp timbre (m.)
start (vb.) commencer sec. 81
station gare, station (f.)
stay (vb.) rester
stewardess hôtesse de l'air
still encore, toujours
stop s'arrêter, cesser
storekeeper commercant (m), -e (f.)
store window vitrine (f.)
straight ahead tout droit
street rue (f.)
street map plan (m.)
student étudiant (m.) ,-e (f.)
study (vb.) étudier

stylish chic
succeed réussir
sugar sucre *(m.)*
suit costume *(m.)*
suitcase valise *(f.)*
sun soleil *(m.)*
sunglasses lunettes *(f.)* de soleil
supermarket supermarché *(m.)*
surprise *(vb.)* surprendre *(irreg.)*
   sec. 29
sure sûr
survey enquête *(f.)*
swim nager, se baigner
swimming pool piscine *(f.)*

tablet comprimé *(m.)*
take prendre *(irreg.) sec. 29*
   take down descendre
   take part participer
   take place avoir lieu
   take up monter
tall grand
tape recorder magnétophone *(m.)*
tea thé *(m.)*
telegram télégramme *(m.)*
telephone *(vb.)* téléphoner
telephone booth cabine *(f.)*
   téléphonique
tell dire *(irreg.) page 117*
tent tente *(f.)*
terrible affreux
thank remercier
that/this *sec. 12, 56*
theft vol *(m.)*
their leur, leurs
there là, y
these/those *sec. 12, 56*
think penser
thirsty, to be thirsty avoir soif
ticket billet *(m.)*
time temps *(m.)*; heure *(f.)*;
   fois *(f.)*
timetable horaire *(m.)*
tip (gratuity) pourboire *(m.)*
tire pneu *(m.)*
tired fatigué

today aujourd'hui
toilet toilettes *(f. pl.)*
tomorrow demain
too trop
too much/many trop (de)
tooth dent *(f.)*
towel serviette *(f.)*
town ville *(f.)*
train train *(m.)*
train station gare *(f.)*
translation traduction *(f.)*
travel *(vb.)* voyager *sec. 81*
truck camion *(m.)*
try *(vb.)* essayer *sec. 81*

ugly laid
umbrella parapluie *(m.)*
unable: unable to pay je ne peux
   pas payer
under sous
understand comprendre *(irreg.)*
   sec. 29
unemployed en/au chômage
unfair injuste
unfortunately malheureusement
unhappy malheureux
United States États-Unis *(m. pl.)*
until jusqu'à, jusqu'à ce que
upstairs en haut
usually d'habitude
use *(vb.)* utiliser

VCR magnétoscope *(m.)*
vacancies (hotel) chambres
   libres
vacate (room) libérer
vacation vacances *(f.pl.)*
valid valable
valuables objets *(m. pl.)* de
   valeur
vegetable légume *(m.)*
view vue *(f.)*
   view over the sea vue sur mer
visit *(vb.)* visiter

wait (for) attendre
waiter garçon(*m.*)
waitress serveuse *(f.)*
wake up réveiller, se réveiller
Wales pays *(m.)* de Galles
walk *(vb.)* marcher
   to go for a walk se promener
   sec. 81
wallet porte-feuille *(m.)*
want *(vb.)* vouloir *(irreg.) sec. 48*
warm, to be warm avoir chaud
wash *(vb.)* laver, se laver
watch *(vb.)* regarder
watch over surveiller
watch (wrist) montre *(f.)*
water eau *(f.)*
   drinking water eau potable
waterskiing ski *(m.)* nautique
wave vague *(f.)*
wear *(vb.)* porter
week semaine *(f.)*
well bien
Welsh gallois
west ouest *(m.)*
what *sec. 15, 58*
wheel roue *(f.)*
when quand
where où
which *sec. 15, 52*

who, whom *sec. 15, 52*
why pourquoi
wife femme
wind vent *(m.)*
windsurfing planche *(f.)* à voile
wine vin *(m.)*
wish *(vb.)* désirer, souhaiter
wonderful magnifique
word mot *(m.)*
work *(vb.)* travailler;
   (of machines) marcher
write écrire *(irreg.) page 108*
writing paper papier *(m.)* à
   lettres
wrong: to be wrong avoir tort

yard jardin *(m.)*
year an *(m.)*
yesterday hier
young jeune
your *sec. 19*
yours *sec. 57*

French – English

accord *(m.)* agreement
je suis d'accord I agree
acheter to buy *sec. 81*
actrice actress
addition *(f.)* bill
adresse *(f.)* address
aéroglisseur *(m.)* hovercraft
affaire *(f.)* matter
c'est une bonne affaire it's a
  bargain (good buy)
affaires *(f. pl.)* business
homme d'a. businessman
femme d'a. businesswoman
affreux awful
afin de in order to
agence *(f.)* agency
agréable pleasant
aider to help
aimable kind
aimer to like, to love
alcool *(m.)* alcohol
Allemagne *(f.)* Germany
allemand German
aller *(irreg.)* to go *pages 93/94*
allumette *(f.)* match (light)
ambassade *(f.)* embassy
ambulance *(f.)* ambulance
ambulancier *(m.)*, **-ière** *(f.)*
  ambulance driver
améliorer to improve
amener to bring *sec. 81*
américain American
Amérique *(f.)* America
ami *(m.)*, **-e** *(f.)* friend
amuser to amuse
s'amuser to enjoy oneself
an *(m.)* year
analyser to analyze
anglais English
Angleterre *(f.)* England
annonce *(f.)* advertisement
annoncer to announce *sec. 81*
annuler to cancel
antiquaire *(m. & f.)* antique
  dealer
appareil *(m.)* machine
appareil-photo *(m.)* camera
appartement *(m.)* apartment
appeler1 to call *sec. 81*
s'appeler to be called
apporter to bring
apprécier to appreciate
apprendre *(irreg.)* to learn *sec. 29*
approuver to approve (*of*)
après after
après-midi *(m. or f.)* afternoon
argent *(m.)* money
arrêter, s'arrêter to stop
arriver to arrive; to happen
ascenseur *(m.)* elevator
asseoir, s'asseoir *(irreg.)* to sit
  down *page 167*
assez enough; fairly
astronaute *(m. & f.)* astronaut
attacher to attach
attendre to wait (for)
au-dessus de above
augmenter to increase
augmentation *(f.)* increase
aujourd'hui today
au revoir good-bye
aussi also
aussitôt que as soon as
autant (de) as much/many
autobus *(m.)* bus
automobiliste *(m. & f.)* motorist
autoroute *(f.)* highway
autre other
avance: à l'avance in advance
avant before
avion *(m.)* airplane

avis *(m.)* opinion
à mon avis in my opinion
avocat *(m.)*, -e *(f.)* lawyer
avoir *(irreg.)* to have sec 4
avoir lieu to take place

bagages *(m. pl.)* luggage
baigner: se b. to swim
bain *(m.)* bath
banque *(f.)* bank
banquier *(m.)*, -ière *(f.)* banker
bar *(m.)* bar
bas, basse *(f.)* low
en bas downstairs
bateau *(m.)* boat
beau *chapter 6* beautiful
beaucoup (de) much/many
Belgique *(f.)* Belgium
bibliothèque *(f.)* library
bicyclette *(f.)* bicycle
bien well
bien que (+*subj*) although
bientôt soon
bière *(f.)* beer
bilingue bilingual
billet *(m.)* ticket
bizarre odd
blessé injured
bleu blue
boire *(irreg.)* to drink *page 117*
boîte *(f.)* box
boite de nuit nightclub
bon, bonne *(f.)* good
boucherie *(f.)* butcher's
boulangerie *(f.)* bakery
bouteille *(f.)* bottle
bras *(m.)* arm
britannique British
brochure *(f.)* brochure
brouillard *(m.)* fog
bruit *(m.)* noise
brûler to burn
brun brown
bruyant noisy

cadeau *(m.)* gift
café *(m.)* coffee; café
caisse *(f.)* cash register
calme calm, quiet
cambrioleur *(m.)* burglar
camion *(m.)* truck
camper to camp
Canada *(m.)* Canada
capter to pick up (broadcast)
car *(m.)* coach
carte *(f.)* card; map
carte de crédit credit card
carte postale postcard
casser to break
cathédrale *(f.)* cathedral
ce, cette, etc. this *sec. 12*
celui, celle, etc. the one *sec. 56*
célèbre famous
cesser to stop
chaise *(f.)* chair
chaise longue lounge chair
chambre *(f.)* bedroom
femme de chambre
chambermaid
champ *(m.)* field
chance *(f.)* luck
changer to change
chanter to sing
chapeau *(m.)* hat
chaque each
château *(m.)* castle
chaud hot
avoir chaud to be hot, warm
il fait c. it's warm (weather)
chemise *(f.)* shirt
chemise de nuit nightshirt
chèque *(m.)* check
cher *(m.)*, chère *(f.)* dear
chercher to look for
cheveux *(m. pl.)* hair (on head)
chic *(inv)* stylish
Chine *(f.)* China
choisir to choose
chômage *(m.)* unemployment
en/au chômage unemployed
clé *(f.)* key

client (m.), -e (f.) customer
climatisation (f.) air-conditioning
cœur (m.) heart
coffre-fort (m.) safe (box)
coiffeur (m.), -euse (f.)
 hairdresser
combien how much/many
commander to order
commencer to begin sec. 81
comment how
commerçant (m.), -e(f.)
 storekeeper
compagnie (f.) aérienne airline
 company
composer (un numéro) to dial
comprendre (irreg.) to
 understand sec. 29
comprimé (m.) tablet
compris included
conduire (irreg.) to drive
 chapter 7
conférence (f.) conference; lecture
confirmer to confirm
confiture (f.) jam
confortable comfortable
connaître (irreg.) to know sec. 55
conseiller to advise
construire (irreg.) to build
 page 176
consulter to consult
content pleased
continuer to continue
contrat (m.) contract
copier to copy
correct correct
corriger to correct (sec. 81)
costume (m.) suit
côté (m.) side
 à côté de next to
couleur (f.) color
couper to cut
courageux brave
courrier (m.) mail
courses (f. pl.) shopping
court short
couteau (m.) knife

coûter to cost
crayon (m.) pencil
créer to create
critiquer to criticize
cuillère (f.) spoon
cuir (m.) leather
cuisine (f.) kitchen; cooking

dame lady
dangereux dangerous
danser to dance
date (f.) date
débarquer to disembark
décider to decide
décourager to discourage sec. 81
défendre to defend; to forbid
déjà already
déjeuner (m.) lunch
 petit déjeuner breakfast
délicieux delicious
demain tomorrow
demander to ask (for)
dent (f.) tooth
dentiste (m. & f.) dentist
départ (m.) departure
dépêcher se. d. to hurry
dépenser to spend (money)
depuis since
déranger to disturb
dernier last
derrière behind
descendre to go down; to take
 down
désirer to wish
désolé sorry
détester to hate
devant in front of
devoir (irreg.) to have to (must)
 sec 48
dictionnaire (m.) dictionary
difficile difficult
diner (m.) dinner
diplôme (m.) diploma
dire (irreg.) to say, to tell page 117
directeur (m.), -trice (f.) director
discothèque (f.) disco

discuter de to discuss
dispute *(f.)* quarrel
  se disputer to quarrel
disque *(m.)* record
disquette *(f.)* floppy disk
distractions *(f. pl.)* entertainment
docteur *(m.)* doctor
dommage: quel dommage what
  a pity
donc so, therefore
donner to give
donner sur to overlook (view)
dormir *(irreg.)* to sleep
  je dors, il dort, n. dormons,
  j'ai dormi
douane *(f.)* customs
douanier *(m.),* -**ière** *(f.)* customs
  officer
douleur *(f.)* pain
douter to doubt
drapeau *(m.)* flag
droit: tout droit straight ahead
droite: à droite on/to the right
du, de la, etc. some *sec.1*

eau *(f.)* water
  eau potable drinking water
écossais Scottish
Écosse *(f.)* Scotland
écouter to listen (to)
écrire to write *page 108*
écriture *(f.)* handwriting
efficace efficient
église *(f.)* church
électricien *(m.)* electrician
électrophone *(m.)* record player
émission *(f.)* broadcast
empêcher to prevent
emploi *(m.)* job
encore again; still; yet
encourager to encourage *sec. 81*
énervant annoying
ennuyeux boring; annoying
  s'ennuyer to be bored *sec. 81*
enquête *(f.)* survey
ensuite afterward

entendre to hear
entre between
entrer to enter
enveloppe *(f.)* envelope
envoyer *(irreg.)* to send *page 97*
épicerie *(f.)* grocer's
erreur *(f.)* mistake
éruption *(f.)* rash (skin)
Espagne *(f.)* Spain
espagnol Spanish
espérer to hope *sec. 81*
essayer to try *sec. 81*
essence *(f.)* gasoline
est *(m.)* east
et and
États-Unis *(m. pl.)* United States
étranger foreign
  à l'étranger abroad
être *(irreg.)* *sec..*
étudiant *(m.),* -**e** *(f.)* student
étudier to study
évident obvious
éviter to avoid
exactement exactly
excellent excellent
excursion *(f.)* excursion
explication *(f.)* explanation
exporter to export

face: en face de opposite
facile easy
facteur *(m.),* -**trice** *(f.)* mailman/
  mailwoman
facture *(f.)* invoice
faim *(f.)* hunger
  avoir faim to be hungry
faire *(irreg.)* to do, to make *sec. 77*
falloir *(irreg.)* to be necessary;
  to need
  il nous faut partir we must leave;
  il nous faut 50 francs we need
  50 francs
famille *(f.)* family
fatigué tired
faut *see* **falloir**
fauteuil *(m.)* armchair

féliciter to congratulate
femme woman; wife
fermer to shut
fièvre *(f.)* fever
fille daughter
  jeune fille girl
film *(m.)* film
fils son
fin *(f.)* end
finir to finish
fois *(f.)* time (occasion)
fort strong; loud
fourchette *(f.)* fork
frais *(m.)* **fraîche** *(f.)* fresh
français French
France *(f.)* France
frapper to knock
frère brother
froid cold
  avoir froid to be cold
  il fait f. it's cold (weather)
fromage *(m.)* cheese
fruit(s) *(m.)* fruit
fumer to smoke

gagner to win; earn
gallois Welsh
gant *(m.)* glove
garage *(m.)* garage
garantir to guarantee
garçon boy; waiter
garder to keep
gare *(f.)* train station
gâteau *(m.)* cake
gauche: à gauche on/to the left
généralement generally
gens *(m. pl.)* people
glace *(f.)* ice; ice cream
gouvernement *(m.)* government
grand big, tall
Grande-Bretagne *(f.)* Britain
grave serious
Grèce *(f.)* Greece
gris gray
groupe *(m.)* group
guide *(m.)* guide; guidebook

habiter to live
habitude *(f.)* habit
  d'habitude usually
haut high
  en haut upstairs
heure *(f.)* hour
  heures supplémentaires overtime
heureux happy
heureusement fortunately
hier yesterday
homme man
hôpital *(m.)* hospital
horaire *(m.)* timetable
hôtel *(m.)* hotel
hôtesse de l'air stewardess
huile *(f.)* oil
humeur *(f.)* mood

ici here
il y a there is/are; ago
important important
importer to import
impossible impossible
impressionnant impressive
incendie *(m.)* fire
infirmier *(m.)*, **-ière** *(f.)* nurse
ingénieur *(m.)* engineer
injuste unfair
instant *(m.)* moment
intéressant interesting
interprète *(m. & f.)* interpreter
inviter to invite
irlandais Irish
Irlande *(f.)* Ireland

jamais, ne [verb] **jamais** never
jambe *(f.)* leg
jambon *(m.)* ham
Japon *(m.)* Japan
japonais Japanese
jardin *(m.)* yard
jeune young
joli pretty
jouer to play
journal *(m.)* newspaper

journaliste *(m. & f.)* journalist
jupe *(f.)* skirt
jusqu'à as far as; until

là there
lac *(m.)* lake
laid ugly
lait *(m.)* milk
lampe *(f.)* lamp
langue *(f.)* tongue; language
laver to wash
se laver to wash oneself
leçon *(f.)* lesson
légume vegetable
lentement slowly
lettre *(f.)* letter
leur their *sec. 19*
  le leur theirs *sec. 57*
lever to raise *sec. 81*
  se lever to get up
libérer to free, vacate
librairie *(f.)* bookstore
libre free
licence *(f.)* degree (univ.)
lire *(irreg.)* to read *sec. 80*
lit *(m.)* bed
livre *(m.)* book
livre *(f.)* pound
logiciel *(m.)* software (comput.)
loi *(f.)* law
loin far, long
long *(m.),* **longue** *(f.)* long
louer to rent
lourd heavy
lunettes *(f. pl.)* spectacles
  lunettes de soleil sunglasses

machine *(f.)* machine
magasin *(m.)* store
magnétophone *(m.)* tape
  recorder
magnétoscope *(m.)* VCR
magnifique wonderful
main *(f.)* hand
maintenant now
mais but
maison *(f.)* house

mal badly
malade ill
maladie *(f.)* illness
  malade de la "vache folle"
  "mad cow" disease
malheureux unhappy
malheureusement unfortunately
Manche *(f.)* Channel
manger to eat *sec. 81*
marchander to haggle
marché *(m.)* market
Marché commun Common
  Market
marcher to walk
mari husband
mariage *(m.)* marriage
marié married
marier: se marier to get married
marque *(f.)* brand
match *(m.)* match (sport)
matin *(m.)* morning
mauvais bad
mécanicien *(m.)* mechanic
médecin *(m.)* doctor
médicament *(m.)* medicine
meilleur *(adj.)* better
même same; even
mer *(f.)* sea
mère mother
message *(m.)* message
méthode *(f.)* method
mettre *(irreg.)* to put *sec. 30*
midi *(m.)* midday
mien, le mien mine *sec. 57*
mieux better
minuit *(m.)* midnight
mode *(f.)* fashion
moderne modern
moi me
  avec/pour moi with/for me
moins less
mois *(m.)* month
moitié *(f.)* half
mon, ma, mes my *sec. 19*
montagne *(f.)* mountain
monter to go up; to take up
montre *(f.)* watch

montrer to show
mouchoir (m.) handkerchief
mot (m.) word
  un petit mot a note
moteur (m.) engine
moto (f.) motorbike
musée (m.) museum
musique (f.) music

nager to swim sec. 81
nécessaire necessary
neiger to snow sec. 81
nettoyer to clean sec. 81
neuf (m.), neuve (f.) new
neveu nephew
nez (m.) nose
nièce niece
nom (m.) name
non no
nord (m.) north
normal normal
note (f.) bill
notre, nos our sec. 19
  le nôtre ours sec. 57
nourriture (f.) food
nouveau new sec. 27
nouvelle(s) (f.) news
nuit (f.) night
  boîte (f.) de nuit nightclub
numéro (m.) number

obéir to obey
obtenir (irreg.) to obtain page 167
occasion (f.) opportunity
  une voiture d'o. a used car
occupé busy
offenser to offend
offre (f.) offer
opéra (m.) opera
ordinaire ordinary
ordinateur (m.) computer
ordonnance (f.) prescription
organiser to organize
ou or
où where
oublier to forget

ouest (m.) west
ouvrir (irreg.) to open
  j'ouvre, il ouvre,
  n. ouvrons, j'ai ouvert
ouvert (adj.) open

pain (m.) bread
  pain grillé toast
panne (f.) break down
papier (m.) paper
  papier à lettres writing paper
parapluie (m.) umbrella
parc (m.) park
parce que because
pardonner to forgive
parfum (m.) perfume
parler to speak
participer to take part
partir (irreg.) to leave page 55
partout everywhere
passeport (m.) passport
passer to spend (time)
patiner to skate
patinoire (f.) skating rink
patron (m.), -onne (f.) owner,
  boss
pauvre poor
payer to pay (for) sec. 81
  p. en espèces to pay in cash
pays (m.) country
pays (m.) de Galles Wales
pêche (f.) peach
pêche (f.) fishing
  aller à la pêche to go fishing
peindre (irreg.) to paint page 128
pellicule (f.) film (for snapshots)
penser to think
perdre to lose
père father
perfectionner to perfect
permettre (irreg.) to allow sec. 30
permis (m.) licence
  p. de conduire driver's license
personne (f.) person
  ne [verb] personne no one
persuader to persuade

petit small
peut-être perhaps
pharmacie *(f.)* drugstore
photo *(f.)* photograph
  prendre en p. to take a photo
pièce *(f.)* **d'identité** identification
piscine *(f.)* swimming pool
place *(f.)* place, seat; square
plage *(f.)* beach
plainte *(f.)* complaint
plaire *(irreg.)* to please *page 150*
  s'il vous plaît please
plaisir *(m.)* pleasure
plan *(m.)* street map
planche *(f.)* **à voile** windsurfing
  board
  faire de la planche à voile
  to windsurf
plat *(m.)* dish
plein full
pleuvoir *(irreg.)* to rain
  il pleut it's raining
  il a plu it rained
plonger to dive
plus more
  ne [verb] **plus** no more/no
  longer
plusieurs several
pneu *(m.)* tire
poche *(f.)* pocket
poisson *(m.)* fish
poissonnerie *(f.)* fish market
poli polite
police *(f.)* police
  un agent de police police officer
pomme *(f.)* apple
  pomme de terre potato
pompier *(m.)* firefighter
port *(m.)* port, harbor
porte-feuille *(m.)* wallet
porte-monnaie *(m.)* purse
porter to carry; to wear
possible possible
poste *(m.)* job
poste *(f.)* post office
pour for; in order to

pourboire *(m.)* tip (gratuity)
pourquoi why
pouvoir *(irreg.)* to be able (can)
  sec. 48
pratiquer to practice
préférer to prefer *sec. 81*
premier first
prendre *(irreg.)* to take *sec. 29*
préparer to prepare
près de near
président-directeur général
  chairman and managing
  director
presse *(f.)* press
  conférence de presse press
  conference
prêt ready
principal main
prix *(m.)* price
probable probable
prochain next
produit *(m.)* product
profession *(f.)* profession
profond deep
projet *(m.)* plan
promener to take for a walk
  sec. 81
  se promener to go for a walk
promettre *(irreg.)* to promise
  sec. 30
promotion *(f.)* special offer
psychologie *(f.)* psychology
publicité *(f.)* advertising
puisque since, because

qualité *(f.)* quality
quand when
que *(interrog)* what
que *(rel. pron.)* whom/which
  sec. 52
quel which/what *sec. 58*
quelque chose something
question *(f.)* question
  poser une question to ask a
  question

queue *(f.)* line
  faire la queue to line up
qui *(interrog)* who
qui *(rel. pron.)* who/which
quitter to leave
quoique *(+ subj)* although

radio *(f.)* radio
rage *(f.)* rabies
raison *(f.)* reason
  avoir raisin to be right
raisonnable reasonable
rapidement quickly
raser to shave
  se raser to shave oneself
rasoir *(m.)* razor
récemment recently
recevoir *(irreg.)* to receive
  je reçois, il reçoit,
  nous recevons,
  ils reçoivent, j'ai reçu,
  je recevrai
recommender to recommend
refuser to refuse
regarder to look (at), watch
régime *(m.)* diet
régler to settle *sec. 81*
regretter to regret
reine queen
remercier to thank
remplir to fill
rencontrer to meet
rendez-vous *(m.)* appointment
rendre to give back
renseignment(s) information
rentrer to return
réparer to repair
repas *(m.)* meal
répéter to repeat *sec. 81*
répondre to reply
reporter *(m.)* reporter (news)
reporter to take back; postpone
reposer, se reposer to rest
réserver to book
restaurant *(m.)* restaurant
rester to stay

retard *(m.)* lateness
  en retard late
retourner to return
réunion *(f.)* meeting
réussir to succeed
réveiller, se réveiller to wake up
revenu *(m.)* income
revue *(f.)* magazine
rhume *(m.)* cold
  rhume des foins hay fever
riche rich
rien: ne [verb] rien nothing
robe *(f.)* dress
roue *(f.)* wheel
rouler to drive
rue *(f.)* street
russe Russian
Russie *(f.)* Russia

sable *(m.)* sand
sac *(m.)* bag
  sac à main pocketbook
  sac de couchage sleeping bag
salade *(f.)* salad
salaire *(m.)* salary
sale dirty
salle *(f.)* room
santé *(f.)* health
savoir *(irreg.)* to know *sec. 48*
secrétaire *(m. & f.)* secretary
semaine *(f.)* week
serveuse *(f.)* waitress
serviette *(f.)* napkin; towel;
  briefcase
servir *(irreg.)* to serve *page 145*
seul alone; only
seulement only
sida *(m.)* Aids
sien, le sien his/hers/its *sec. 57*
signer to sign
ski *(m.)* skiing
  ski nautique waterskiing
  faire du ski to go skiing
sœur sister
soif *(f.)* thirst
  avoir soif to be thirsty

soir *(m.)* evening
soldes *(m. pl.)* sales (bargains)
soleil *(m.)* sun
lunettes *(f. pl.)* de soleil
sunglasses
son, sa, ses his/her/its *sec. 19*
sortie *(f.)* exit
sortie de secours fire exit
sortir *(irreg.)* to go out; to take out
page 167
souhaiter to wish
soupe *(f.)* soup
sous under
souvenir *(m.)* souvenir; memory
se souvenir de *(conj. like venir)*
to remember
souvent often
spectacle *(m.)* show
sport *(m.)* sport
stylo *(m.)* pen
stylo bille ballpoint pen
sucre *(m.)* sugar
sud *(m.)* south
supermarché *(m.)* supermarket
supplément *(m.)* extra
sur on
sûr sure
surprendre *(irreg.)* to surprise
sec. 29
surtout especially
surveiller to watch over

taille *(f.)* size; waist
tant (de) so much/many
tante aunt
tasse *(f.)* cup
télégramme *(m.)* telegram
téléphone *(m.)* telephone
téléphoner to telephone
cabine téléphonique telephone
booth
temps *(m.)* time
de temps en temps occasionally
tension *(f.)* stress; blood pressure
tente *(f.)* tent
terre *(f.)* land

tête *(f.)* head
thé *(m.)* tea
tien, le tien yours *sec. 57*
timbre *(m.)* stamp
toilettes *(f. pl.)* toilet
tomber to fall
t. en panne to break down
ton, ta, tes your *sec. 19*
tort: avoir tort to be wrong
tôt early
toujours always; still
tout all *page 94*
tout le monde everyone
tout de suite immediately
tout everything
traduction *(f.)* translation
train *(m.)* train
travailler to work
traverser to cross
triste sad
tromper to deceive
se tromper to make a mistake
trop too
trop (de) too much/many
trouver to find

Union *(f.)* européenne European
Union
urgence *(f.)* emergency
en cas d'urgence in an
emergency
utiliser to use

vacances *(f. pl.)* holidays
vague *(f.)* wave
valable valid
valeur *(f.)* value
objets de valeur valuables
valise *(f.)* suitcase
faires ses valises to pack
vélo *(m.)* bike
vendre to sell
venir *(irreg.)* to come *pages 93/94*
vent *(m.)* wind
vente *(f.)* sale
vérifier to check

verre *(m.)* glass
verser to pour; to pay
  verser des arrhes *(f. pl.)* to leave
  a deposit
veste *(f.)* jacket
vestibule *(m.)* hall
vêtements *(m. pl.)* clothes
viande *(f.)* meat
vie *(f.)* life
vieux old *sec. 27*
ville *(f.)* town
vin *(m.)* wine
visiter to visit
vitrine *(f.)* store window
vivre *(irreg.)* to live *page 185*

voici here is/are
voile *(f.)* sail
  faire de la voile to go sailing
voir *(irreg.)* to see *chapter 11*
voisin *(m.)*, -e *(f.)* neighbor
voiture *(f.)* car
vol *(m.)* flight; theft
vôtre your *sec. 19*
vôtre, le vôtre yours *sec. 57*
vouloir *(irreg.)* to want *sec. 48*
voyager to travel
vue *(f.)* view

Index

The numbers refer to section headings unless pages are specified